CALL ME ADIRONDACK

CALL ME
ADIRONDACK

Murray Heller

CALL ME ADIRONDACK:
NAMES AND THEIR STORIES

Library of Congress Cataloging-in-Publication Data

Heller, Murray.
    Call me Adirondack : names and their stories
        p.   cm.
    Bibliography: p.
    Includes indexes.
    ISBN: 0–918517–14–1
    1. Names, Geographical—New York (State)—Adirondack Mountains.   2. Adirondack Mountains (N.Y.)—History, Local.
I. Title.
F127.A2H66   1989
974.7'53—dc19   89–768   CIP

The CHAUNCY PRESS

SARANAC LAKE, NEW YORK 12983

To

ALLEN WALKER READ

Teacher and Friend, whose vision of human possibilities
is equalled only by his love of human decency.

Contents

Foreward 9

Acknowledgements 11

1. A Good Name is Hard to Find 13

2. What Kind of a Name is That? 27

3. There is Nothing Like a Name 35

4. The Rorschäch Test 47

5. Digging with Names 67

6. That's a Folktale! 79

7. Mirror, Mirror on the Map 87

8. A Babble of Names 99

9. A Pond by Any Other Name 119

10. That's No Fit Name For A Name! 133

11. Where Do We Go From Here 141

Index of Names and Places 151

Index of Maps and Schematics 163

Selected Reading 165

Foreword

We are a curious bunch, we humans. We like to know where we are and when we are there, not to mention the inexorable who we are. But we best leave the "who we are" to the philosopher and theologian in us, just as we leave the when and where to our watches and maps.

Our curiosity is boundless, and that's one of our pervasively endearing, if at times dangerous, qualities. And most often the satisfaction of our curiosity gives us deep pleasure. All of us have experienced that internal glow as we "got it," some bit of information or some idea, something that piqued our interest, scratched our curiosity bone. From the earliest of times, to gain information, to learn something, has been also to experience pleasure.

Nowhere is this more evident than in the incessant "why?" of children. And in few places can the "whys" be more enjoyably, and, I might add, more harmlessly satisfied than when answering, as one follows the little finger tracing along on the travel map, "why is it called that?"

This book aims to inform and therefore to please. The pages that follow describe how and when and why some places in the Adirondacks got their names.

You'll read about what baptismal fires they may have gone through or what folk humor prevailed. You'll learn what some names "mean" and why what some names "mean" really doesn't mean anything anymore. This book aims, echoing antiquity, to instruct and to delight.

You will not find an exhaustive, or for that matter exhausting, encyclopedic and definitive listing of all Adirondack place names and their etymologies. Such a book is needed, and I'm sure will be produced. But our journey through the Adirondacks aims at other pleasures and other information. We'll be looking at the kinds of names we have and the kinds of people who first used them.

You will become familiar with a little of the history and folklore, that is, with the human experiences, of those who made the Adirondacks their home. And the stories you read in these pages about our Adirondack place names are just that—stories. Like all folklore, these tales of Adirondack names *touch* upon the truth in important ways: certainly in the ways of documented accuracy which history demands, but even more profoundly in the ways of inspired revelations at the heart of human experiences. Although our fish's tail might stretch in the telling (our Adirondack brook trout might begin to look like whales or at least Lake Champlain "Champs"), we're always true to the spirit as well as the species. These tales are the coin of the realm.

And I am sure, as you move across the Adirondacks, by car or boat or foot—or even by map plotted with your finger—that the knowledge of and about the places you visit will give you pleasure in the knowing.

Murray Heller
Lake Placid
May, 1989

Acknowledgements

My thanks, first of all, to North Country Community College for the Leave which enabled me to complete this book, and to my students over the years who have added to my collection of material, enriched my understanding of the Adirondacks and encouraged my love of its history.

Numerous individuals have generously responded to my requests, among whom the following are especially noted: Jerold Pepper, Librarian at the Adirondack Museum; James Corsaro at Manuscript and Special Collections, New York State Library; and, of extraordinary help, Patrick McIntyre, Head Librarian, North Country Community College. My thanks also to the staff at the New York State Archives.

My thanks to the *Adirondack Daily Enterprise* and the *Lake Placid News.* I am grateful to Mr. Henry Savarie for his schematics and to the Adirondack Park Agency for use of the map of the Adirondack Park. Excerpt from *Names On The Land,* by George R. Stewart, copyright 1945, 1958 by George R. Stewart; copyright renewed 1972 by George R. Stewart. Reprinted with permission of Houghton-Mifflin Co.

To those willing to read and comment upon the early drafts, my deepest gratitude. Their critical insights and suggestions give the book much of its strength; its weaknesses are mine alone. The responses of Mr. Neal Burdick of St. Lawrence University, Mrs. Elizabeth Goldsmith of Broadstairs, England, Professor Michael Kudish of Paul Smith's College, and Mr. Roger Ziman of New York City were extremely helpful to me.

Of special note is my appreciation for the extraordinarily valuable reading done by Professor Phillips Stevens, Jr. of the State University of New York at Buffalo and Editor of *New York Folklore.*

My gratitude to Walt Steesy of Heart of the Lakes Publishing who gave of his advice and skill toward the physical layout and easy readability of the book and to Mrs. Sandra Pope for the preparation of the manuscript. Her patient humor and proficiency sustained both of us through innumerable revisions.

And most profound thanks of all to my wife, Madge. Her support has made this book possible.

1

A Good Name Is Hard To Find

If you took one of those hot air balloon rides out of Glens Falls and if the balloon rose high enough, you'd believe what lay below was an island. From that height, the Adirondacks resemble nothing so much as a grandly mountainous island. On the north and northwest the St. Lawrence River marks its coast, just as Lake Champlain measures its eastern slope. The Mohawk River traces the southern edge, even as it hints at the Black River and Lake Ontario to the west. Within this island lies the magnificent Adirondack Park: six million acres of grandeur and beauty. To help visualize its magnitude, consider that this "park" corresponds in size to all of the neighboring state of Vermont. It is the largest, and to me the grandest, of all the state parks in the United States.

The natural beauty of the Adirondacks and its gifts of mountains and waters are extraordinary enough, but note this: New York City is only 200 miles to the south, Boston a bit more to the east. The populations of The Big Apple and Beantown could leave after breakfast and be in the Adirondacks before lunch. Quebec, Montreal and Ottawa are neighbors, only a few hours' car ride from the north; Albany, the state capital, Utica, Syracuse and Buffalo fringe our southern and western rim. Indeed, over 60 million Americans and Canadians can drive from their homes in the morning and sleep that evening under Adirondack stars. Remarkable!

The Adirondacks have always been remarkable. The people and nations of the Iroquois created, in the Adirondacks long before the white man came, a political institution, a confederacy, which was the envy of our founding fathers and the model of our own Constitution. The Adirondack region was the arena for some of the most crucial confrontations between France and England when our destiny was being decided. It saw bloody battles of the Revolutionary War and its sequel, the War of 1812, when our nationhood was being decided. The Adirondacks watched Alexander Hamilton and Aaron Burr speculating for land long before they fought their famous duel. The Adirondacks heard no less a personage than George Washington, while trying to buy up a tract of land, exclaim that it was the gateway to the empire! That's why New Yorkers are citizens of The Empire State.

Scratch the surface of the Adirondacks and you'll find a pioneer and woodsman from whom our first American novelist, James Fenimore Cooper, drew his Deerslayer, Natty Bumppo. The Adirondacks knew Teddy Roosevelt as president first, as he was rushed down from its highest peaks by Adirondack guides to take the oath of office upon McKinley's assassination. The Adirondacks afforded inspiration and serenity to Ralph Waldo Emerson and others of the intellectual, literary and religious "Brahmin" Bostonians. Our mountains offered refuge to victims of the Civil War period, especially fugitive slaves and militant abolitionists; indeed, it is in North Elba, on his farm near Lake Placid, that the body of John Brown finally did come to rest.

The Adirondacks hosted the summer "camps" of the likes of Rockefeller, Vanderbilt, Morgan; but these paragons of successful private enterprise had to share the glories of the Adirondacks with such unsavory figures as the New York underworld's "Legs" Diamond and "Dutch" Schultz. Yes the Adirondacks absorbs us all and has room for Mark Twain and Robert Louis Stevenson, Norman Bethune and Albert Einstein, Bela Bartok and Leonard Bernstein. On the stage of a local Saranac Lake movie house, Al Jolson and Eddie Cantor danced and sang; this, years after "Westerns" were shot in the vicinity and many silent screen actors and cameramen retired in the Will Rogers complexes just outside of the village.

Scratch a bit deeper and we'll find Napoleon's brother! Here in the Adirondacks Joseph Bonaparte, brother to the emperor and former king of Spain spent many a pleasant day with his Philadelphia Main Line mistress. Dig a bit deeper and we'll find the scene on a summer's lake where the dreams of a young man and his pregnant girlfriend came to grief and became the drama for Theodore Dreiser's *An American Tragedy.*

Dig even a bit deeper and we'll be told that the Adirondacks represent one of the oldest of land masses on the face of the earth. Is it any wonder that this is a remarkable land? And is it any wonder that it searched for a suitable name, trying on and discarding one after another for more than three hundred years before the right one came along?

The very first recorded name given to that which included what we know as the Adirondacks appears first as far back as 1497, just a few years after Columbus's landfall in the Indies. Our recording is by that other great traveler of the time, John Cabot. Coming to the coast of Labrador, Cabot named the entirety of the new world he found "Prima Vista," that is, a first look. Cabot meant "Prima Vista" to include the Laurentian or Canadian Shield in what is now Canada, all of what we call New England, and our Adirondacks. Although Cabot did not actually "see" the Adirondacks and have our mountains in mind, "Prima Vista" is a perfect name with which to start our nation and our story.

The land waited for two generations before Jacques Cartier discovered the estuary of a great river and dropped anchor in the waters which he named after the saint upon whose day in that year 1535 landfall was made. Thus on August 10, St. Lawrence's Day, giving thanks for a safe landing, Cartier was to bequeath upon the new world a name for a mighty river and a major geologic region as well as a county in New York State.

By this time, Prima Vista had already given way to more obvious French claims in the New World. As Spain had created her New Spain and England her New England, so now France claimed her New France. That part of New France which contained the Adirondacks was called "Avacal." (see page 17)

By 1600, French explorers and early settlers had looked upon the mountain ranges to the south from their settlements on the north side of the St. Lawrence River, and, anticipating the same sort of gold and silver deposits already discovered in South America, dubbed the great northern range the "Peruvian" or "Peru" mountains. This name lingered through the first half of the 1600s, and even today it remains with us, without the gold and silver, in Peru Bay on Lake Champlain and, just inland from there, the town and the hamlet of Peru, pronounced locally, by the way, as "Pru." I have been told, however, that it was the Yankees who around 1790 gave Peru its exotic flavor.

From "Prima Vista" to "Avacal," part of "New France" to "Peruvian" or "Peru" Mountains, it took about a hundred years to create these three names. But the pace picks up after 1600.

By this time, the Dutch West India Company had come to our corner of the New World, and they too created their New Netherlands, their "Novi Belgii." And on their map of 1614, the west side of Lake Champlain is marked "Hodenosauneega," which means in Iroquois, roughly, "People of the Long House." Their 1616 version of the same map uses the term "Iroquoisia" and extends this name, as well as claim, to the east or Vermont side of Lake Champlain, what the Dutch map calls "The Iroquois Ocean." A 1621 edition of this map uses the name "Konoshion," synonymous for "Iroquoisia." (see page 19)

Since the Dutch seem to have limited their land claims to no farther north than around the Albany area despite calling all the territory "Novi Belgii," perhaps their maps reflect accurate recognition of those who had already made claim. If this is so, then the Adirondacks was part of Iroquoian territory and its name, even if not always used by the Iroquois themselves, was "Hodenosauneega," "Iroquoisia" or "Konoshion." One or another of these names could be found on maps for the next 150 years, as late as 1785.

The Dutch gave us one more name for the Adirondacks, but unlike the Catskills, it didn't really fit and was discarded. During the height of Dutch influence in New York, which was ironically the same time English presence was overwhelming it (1630–60), a very popular Dutch figure emerged. Not Peter Stuyvesant of New York City fame but Arendt van Curler, head of the Rensselaerswick colony. He was well liked by the Mohawk, who gave his name to political offices as well as places. He was so respected that the Mohawk called all future governors

From Abraham Ortelius's *Theatrum Orbis Terrarum*, 1575

"Corlear" and the mountain ranges to the north the "Corlear Mountains." But these names didn't take, especially with the British, although we do have Corlear Bay on Lake Champlain.

During this same period, the mid-1600s, French exploration continued north and west of the Adirondacks. A Jesuit missionary, Simon Le Moyne, recorded a journey he took west from Montreal. He notes a high range of mountains which most likely were the northwestern extent of the Adirondacks, and in his journal, part of the Jesuit Relations for 1653–1654, names these the "St. Margaret Mountains." Although this name, like "Corlear Mountains," did not root itself very well, a close cousin seems to have hung on till as late as 1877, some hundred years, for the name "Mountains of St. Marthe" is recorded.

With the eclipse of Dutch influence in the Hudson and Mohawk valleys came new maps and new names, this time English. Beverwyck became Albany and Corlear or even the more fitting Hodenosauneega or Iroquoisia were discarded and English taste settled on a descriptive term that highlighted their primary interest in the area.

Gold and silver were not to be found in the Adirondacks, but there were two commodities perhaps even more valuable: timber for the ships of the British Empire's navy, and beaver, millions of them. The fur of the beaver became the currency of exchange, the making of fortunes, the basis of foreign policy, the destiny of nations. The British map-makers of the 1750s scrawled across the vast spaces of the Adirondacks a phrase with a mix of antiquated spelling and a transliterated Native American term, "The Antient Couchsachrage," a beaver-hunting country. (see page 21)

The French, too, thought of the beaver; they named a colony in the Adirondacks "Castorland," *castor* being the French term for beaver. It has been suggested that Couchsachrage means harsh, dismal weather, winter even, and although it seems apt enough, "Beaver Hunting Country" is on the maps next to "Couchsachrage," and that is its generally accepted meaning.

During the cataclysmic period of the last stages of what we call the French and Indian War but is more accurately the French and English Wars, the period of the final conflicts of 1750–1760, the informal name often used by the French was

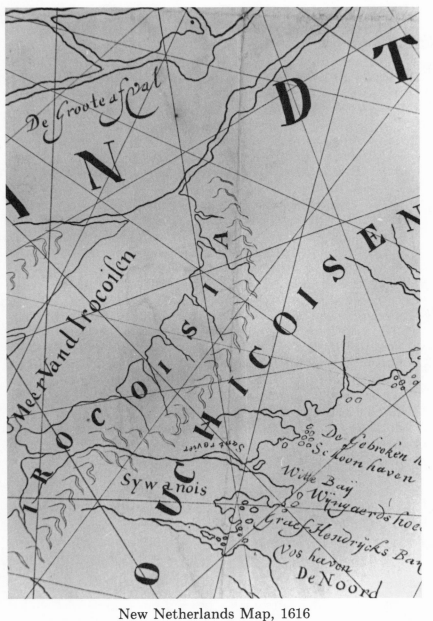

New Netherlands Map, 1616

"The Dismal Wilderness"; even today there is a "Dismal Swamp" in St. Lawrence County. The English, not to be outdone in any way by the French, informally called the Adirondacks "The Dark and Bloody Ground," a name later to be used to describe the horrors of war in Kentucky as well.

Let's go back now and look at the growing mountain of names tried on and discarded by our Adirondacks. At the base of the pile is "Prima Vista," then "Avacal," "Peruvian Mountains," "Novi Belgii," "Hodenosauneega," "Iroquoisia," "Konoshion," "Corlear Mountains," "St. Margaret Mountains," "Mountains of St. Marthe," and, just before the Revolutionary War, "The Antient Couchsachrage," "The Dismal Wilderness" or "The Dark and Bloody Ground."

The end of the War of 1812 saw the Adirondacks blessed with another profusion of names. The hero of the war, for northern New Yorkers, was Major General Alexander Macomb, and his name was briefly immortalized, if such a paradox is possible, as a deep patriotic wave called the peaks "The Macomb Mountains." At the same time, two more informal names gained currency: Canadians and New Yorkers in the St. Lawrence valley called our Adirondacks "The South Woods," while in Albany and farther "downstate" the Adirondacks became known as "The North Woods." This is a prime example of Einstein's law of name relativity. This informal tag lingers on today when we talk about the "North Country."

A more formal and serious contender of a name for the Adirondacks emerged shortly after the upheaval of the War of 1812 subsided. The 1820s witnessed the first of the city sportsmen scouring the Fulton Chain area in search of good hunting. This wonderful land of lakes and ponds and rugged terrain was part of a tract owned by an extremely wealthy Rhode Island merchant, one John Brown. We are not talking of the Great Abolitionist of North Elba, but this John Brown was remarkable in his own right: organizer of Providence's Tea Party to rival Boston's, developer of one of the first of the clipper fleets to trade with China, founder of Rhode Island's Brown University . . . but more about him later.

The 210,000 acres—more or less—(a wonderful Adirondack expression) which included the Fulton Chain was called "Brown's Tract," aptly enough I suppose. Sometimes in their

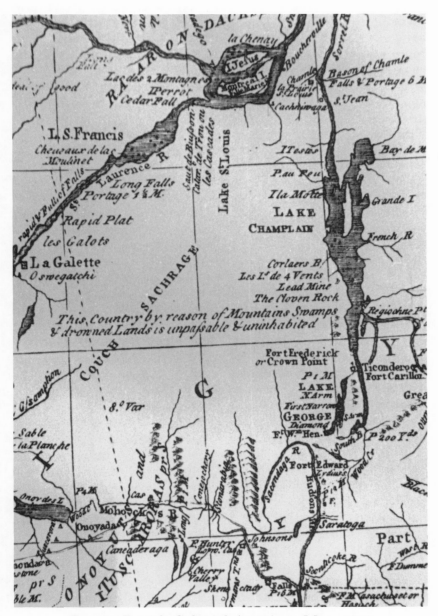

From a British Colonial American Map, 1755

correspondence these wealthy sportsmen used the term
"Northern Wilderness," but this very popular hunting area was
generally known as "Brown's Tract," and this name became
more and more familiar to those who had any interest in the
region. Indeed, since it was the sportsmen from the cities who
wrote about their experiences hunting and fishing the area, all
sorts of documents, notices, letters, and articles in newspapers
and land sales more and more referred to the region as "Brown's
Tract." An almost natural extension followed; all of the
Adirondacks became known by Brown's name, and the peaks
were even referred to as "Brown's Mountains."

The popularity of "Brown's Tract" as the "real" name of
our Adirondacks was widespread, despite the fact that the tract
itself is a quite small portion of the vast expanse of the "North
Country." The two previous major land purchases in the
Adirondacks included well over four million acres, considerably
dwarfing Brown's not quite 210,000. That his name almost won
the day attests to the power of the media even then. Indeed, the
first major attempt at an historical account of the entire
Adirondacks, Sylvester's *Historical Sketches of Northern New
York and The Adirondack Wilderness,* 1877, insists on the name
"Brown's Tract" and launches a lengthy attack upon an upstart
contender. (see page 23)

The more informal and vague "Northern Wilderness"
lingered on through the 1800s and its cousin the "New York
Wilderness" could be seen on many tourist maps. It's interesting
to see the softening of images as we move through this family of
informal names: "The Northern Wilderness" gives way to "The
New York Wilderness" to today's benign "North Country."

To the list of names, which included by the end of all the
wars up through 1812 such shuddering epithets as "The Dark
and Bloody Ground," we can now add these peacetime names of
the 1800s: "Brown's Tract," "Brown's Mountains," "The
Northern Wilderness" and "The New York Wilderness."

But all these names ultimately withdrew from the battle,
some quickly, others more reluctantly when, following Professor
Ebenezer Emmons's ascent of Mount Marcy in August of 1837,
his account was published in the State's Assembly Documents
(#200) of February, 1838. Emmons wrote:

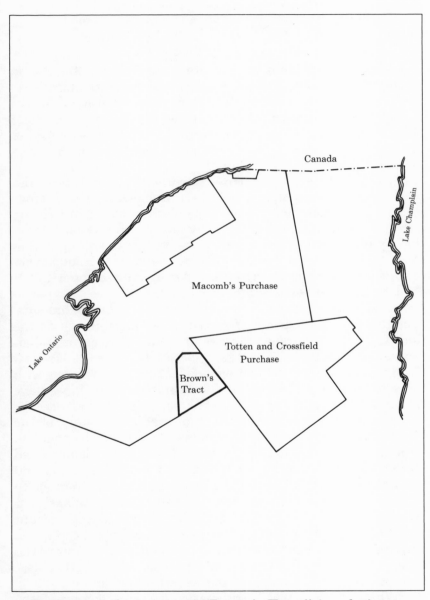

Outlines of the extent of "Brown's Tract" in relation to
"Macomb's Purchase" and "Totten and Crossfield Purchase."

> The cluster of mountains in the neighborhood of the Upper
> Hudson and Ausable rivers, I propose to call the Adirondack
> Group, a name by which a well-known tribe of Indians who
> once hunted here may be commemorated.

Although Emmons was quite specific that the name
"Adirondacks" applied to one range of mountains among others,
and not to the entire region, like the natural extension that was
occurring with "Brown's Tract" at very much the same time
"The Adirondacks" came to mean the entire expanse of
mountains and lakes and valleys of all the land north of the
Mohawk River.

The meaning of the name is shrouded in mystery and
conjecture. Some suggest it is from a Mohawk term, "Aderondackx," for Frenchmen or Englishmen; others note that a Huron
word, "Attiwandaronk," supposedly meant "those who speak a
slightly different language." Also, the Mohawks are reputed to
have called the Hurons "Rondaxes," and the Iroquois are
recorded as referring to any Native American fighting with the
French as a "Rondaxe" or "Arundaks."

Another possibility rests in the Huron word "Arendahronon,"
which referred to a group of Native Americans known as the
Rock Clan. The Huron word, meaning "they of great rocks" or
"those who are great rocks," became for the Mohawk
"Tatirontaks." The "ak" ending means "to eat," and along with
the substitution of the notion of trees instead of rock, we have
"those who eat trees" or our nickname, "The Barkeaters."

And this gives us a clue to that traditional story of the
Mohawk defeating one of the Algonkian tribes foolish enough to
attempt a hunting expedition in the Adirondacks. Bloodied and
scattered, the encroachers were reduced to digging roots and
boiling twigs and bark in the cold and snow of their retreat. In
derision, the Mohawk labelled them "Hatirondaks" or
"Ratirontaks," "those who eat trees." A more sober account
would have it that the term "Ratirontaks" indicated those who
were essentially forest dwellers as opposed to the Iroquois, who
called themselves "Ratinonsionni" or "those who build cabins;"
that is, agricultural people living in settled communities.

Whatever the "true" explanation of the meaning of the
word, the admirably martial and enjoyable "lore," at least from
a Mohawk perspective, captures my imagination and, it seems,

that of most of us in the Adirondacks. We like our "barkeater" story and we wear it with pride.

Perhaps that's partly why we finally chose "The Adirondacks" over "John Brown's Tract." Perhaps also because it's neater to say, not as awkward. Perhaps we didn't really want the "personal" connection, even though both John Browns fought the good fight. Perhaps we were attracted to the romance of the "Indianness" of the sound itself: maybe we picked up on Walt Whitman and felt the syllables roll on our tongues, "AD-I-RON-DACKS." Whatever the reason or combination of reasons, by 1849 travel guides were using the name "Adirondacks" for all of the North Country, and despite the rear guard action fought by "Brown's Tract" and "Northern" or "New York Wilderness," the Adirondacks it was to be, and indeed is.

One more name for our mountains came to us in the last part of the 1800s, when railroads and European politics came facetiously together. It seems that in 1879 a railroad line was laid from Plattsburgh, on Lake Champlain, to Lyon Mountain, about 30 miles west. The notion was to bring the high-grade iron ore from the mines at Lyon Mountain to the lake. There was, and still is, a state penitentiary (now called correctional facility) nearby, at Dannemora, and the generosity of our state officials then, as now also, prompted the offer of prison inmate labor for the building of the rail line. A New York City wit is reported as coupling that generous act with the harsh winters and isolated environment and dubbing the region "The Siberia of North America," a name that might have made the Russian tsar's jailers smile. It didn't make us smile at all, and that dig was quietly buried. Unfortunately, the events of the 1980s have led to this name cropping up again.

Let's take one last look at all our names:

Prima Vista	The Macomb Mountains
Avacal	The South Woods
Peruvian Mountains	The North Woods
Novi Belgii	Hodenosauneega
The Brown's Tract	Iroquoisia
Brown's Mountains	Konoshion
Northern Wilderness	Corlear Mountains
New York Wilderness	St. Margaret Mountains
The North Country	Mountains of St. Marthe
The Adirondack Mountains	The Antient Couchsachrage

The Adirondacks   The Dismal Wilderness
Siberia of North America   The Dark and Bloody Ground

I count 24 all told! Some are informal and tend to be easily dismissed. But we shouldn't do that because they tell their stories as honestly and as importantly as the more formal ones. Some are French, two are of Dutch background, a few Native American, most English. Four different languages and cultures, often kneaded together; the dough from which our names take shape and from which our lives in the Adirondacks rise.

Our names are varied in language and tone, in mood and sensibility, in grand gestures and earthy realism, in formality and flippancy. They tell us about our history, about ourselves. They perhaps hint at our dreams, our unspoken needs, our crucial values. Perhaps it is not so strange that after 400 years (more or less, as the saying goes) we should have settled on a name from the Iroquois, the Mohawk. Perhaps Robert Frost had it right in that the land is not ours till we are the land's.

But while we chew that one over, let's send a card to a friend. You know, the "wish you were here" kind. And post it from COUCHSACHRAGE. And sign it, Your BARKEATER.

And while we wait for an answer, let's figure out all the different kinds of names there are *in* the Adirondacks.

2

What Kind Of A Name Is That?

If there is one thing we can see from looking at the Adirondacks, it is that place-names come in all sizes and shapes. People names do also, and I must admit I never met a place-name as whimsically aspiring as Through-Much-Trial-and-Tribulation-We-Enter-The-Kingdom-Of-Heaven Lindloff, of Clinton County, Iowa, recorded in 1880. Nevertheless, there are some noteworthy specimens of eccentric place-names. There is, for example, the community of Onoville, in central New York, supposedly from the town meeting called to decide upon a name for this newly settled village. After a lengthy and obviously frustrating debate, during which many favorite names were greeted by opponents with cries of "Oh No!," the town fathers, in desperation, called their new settlement, "Onoville."

Closer to home, here in the Adirondacks, we have had names as extraordinary as "Up The River," "Sobriety," and "Bloodville," and still do have such equally wonderful and strange names as "Easy Street," "Sink Hole," and "Grizzle Ocean Pond." A few years back I received a note after a talk I gave at Union College and added the name "Knowersville" to my list of what I call my "Pleasure Names:" those that are surely the children of fancy and zest and the love of a joke. And the letter concluded with this delicious postscript, "Knowersville still has a mayor."

But aside from these funny and strange and eccentric

names, which catch our eye as the unexpected always does, there are literally thousands upon thousands of names in the Adirondacks. The incredible number of places identified and named would bring many happy hours of recording and tabulating to a computer; actually efforts are being made to do just that.

To get a sense of just how many names we have here in our Adirondacks, just consider for a moment the mountain . . . no, the Everest of names which includes all the mountains, peaks, hills, valleys, rivers, streams, brooks, rivulets, lakes, ponds, stillwaters, bogs, swamps, hollows, gullies, woods, farms, meadows, plots, regions, counties, townships, villages, hamlets, highways, roads, lanes, streets, trails, paths and walkways, not to mention the marshes, ridges, forests, mines, parcels, etcetera, etcetera, etcetera . . .

No, it won't do. To list all the names of all the places in the Adirondacks would prove as interesting and informative as the latest issue of the New York City Telephone Directory. Now that is an important and necessary book, but most of us can't get too excited about that kind of reading. No, it won't do. What we need is a system so that we can put lots of names into separate groups, a system that will let us arrange all the names into families so that we can recognize all the relatives in the directory.

One very important and extensive "family" of names represents a gift, a legacy from other peoples before us. And one branch of this "family" grows out of Native American names. It stands to reason that since the Iroquois (especially the Mohawk) were so dominant in the Adirondacks, there are considerably more Iroquoian/Mohawk names than Algonkian. With the help of highly skilled and trained linguists, records of early pioneers and settlers, and information from Mohawk traditionalists, we've been successful in identifying Native American names throughout the Adirondacks, from Saratoga to Ticonderoga to Tahawus to Onchiota to Kiwassa to Schenectady to Oswegatchie to Akwesasne. There are mountains and waterways, villages and cities, streets and woodpaths whose names bear testimony to the Native American heritage in our lives.

We're very possessive of our "Indian" names and proud of them, but whatever the mix of romance and excitement and drama conjured up in a Native American name, the reality is that this branch of the family is a very small minority. In fact, there are not very many Native American names on the landscape.

Another branch of the family, however, has many more offsprings: there are in our Adirondacks a great many names of French descent. They, too, are found throughout the North Country, and, like the Native American names, are sometimes easily recognized and at other times quite disguised. We have the rivers Ausable and perhaps Raquette; there are communities such as Chazy and Castorland; lakes of Champlain and Schroon (yes Schroon Lake is French, even if she doesn't look or sound it).

Although New York City, most of Long Island, the Hudson valley, and the Albany area sport Dutch names in great number, including such internationally recognized places as the Big Apple's "Broadway," Brooklyn's "Coney Island" and where Fort Apache never was, "The Bronx," when you come closer to the North Country you leave Dutch country. You will, however, come to "Watervliet," a curious mix of Dutch and English, just north of Albany. And the legacy of Hudson's ship marks another community, "Half Moon," also a bit north of Albany as you head into the Adirondacks. And there is a "Schuyler Falls," near Plattsburgh, reminding us of the Dutch patroon Van Schuyler. But more of the Dutch later.

Finally, although as with the Dutch, Scottish contributions to our mosaic of names remain for the most part south of the Adirondacks in the Albany area, we do have our own "Loch Bonnie" far north in the mountains as well as "Scotch Bonnet" on Lake George. And the important North Country city of Plattsburgh hints strongly of Scottish presence. When Mr. Platt's settlement was graced with his name, it adopted the Scottish ending "burgh," rather than the English "burg." Thus we have the seat of Clinton County at "Plattsburgh," not at "Plattsburg."

The very few Scottish and Dutch names (that's probably why they stand out), the "feel" of the "old country, old world" French names, and the excitement and poetry of the Native American names join together into a limited but exciting international family of names, which only for convenience's sake we will label "Foreign Names." I don't think this label will hurt if we keep in mind that these names are foreign only to English-speaking people, that there is nothing "foreign" about them at all except in terms of distinguishing them from English. If anyone can suggest a happier word, do let me know and we'll use it. With this in mind, then, we can now leave for the moment our first family or category of names, "Foreign."

In addition to being curious, we humans are often driven by powerful egos. It's not enough to go somewhere or do something; we want everyone else to know that we did it. We are driven to put our name to it. The Adirondacks abound with the names of our discoverers and pioneers and founding settlers, memorials to our hardy ancestors. "Willsboro" and "Elizabethtown" come immediately to mind and recall for us that remarkable man, William Gilliland, of whom we'll hear more later. "Tupper Lake" was initially "Tupper's Lake" for the surveyor who first mapped the region. "Paul Smiths" comes to us thanks to one of our first Adirondack success stories. You know, "poor boy makes good." And he did.

Throughout the Adirondacks and the shadows cast by the mountains, these names and their legacies live with us: "LeRayville," "Plattsburgh," "Gouverneur," "Duane," "Lake Lila," "Bolton's Landing," "Meacham Lake," "Hogansburg," "Keeseville." The list goes on and on, of these men (and a few women) who left, along with other things, their names on the land. These personal names, these names of people who invested their energy, their time and money, their hopes and dreams in the land, these people have left us an immeasurably rich legacy, their names. These "Personal Names" are our second category or family.

A type of name that appeared in the Adirondacks only after Europeans came to the New World is a close cousin of "Personal" Names. Actually they came on the same voyage! These names also refer to people, but whereas "Personal Names" recall those who either lived on the land or were a part of its history in some close, even if humble way, these other "people names" try to make immortal the memory or accomplishments of extraordinary people. And unlike Ozymandias, whose monument crumbled away, names need not worry about winds or rains; names need only remain in the human memory. Thus in the earliest days of our country, as well as in our time (think of all the places now called Kennedy), we commemorate our heroes by placing their names on the geography of our world as well as on the geography of our minds.

While we were winning the Revolutionary War, for example, we had enough energy left over from the fighting to decide that the vast entirety of a chunk of North Country real estate, on the maps as "Charlotte County," after Princess Charlotte, King George's daughter, would not do at all. So we made official proclamation that this huge parcel of land was to be known to all everywhere (or something to that effect) as, you've probably already guessed, "Washington County," comprising all of what is now Warren, Essex, Clinton, Franklin and St. Lawrence Counties as well as the present Washington County.

When we come across "The Fulton Chain," "Franklin County," "Lake Champlain," "Mount Marcy," "Lake Flower," "Lake George," "Rooseveltown," we are witnessing historical tribute to our leaders and heroes. These we call "Commemorative Names." Sometimes we record and commemorate an event rather than a person. "Calamity Pond," "Sabbath Day Point," "Sunday Creek" and "Bloody Pond" refer to events, some gruesome, others trivial, but all commemorative.

A fourth category of names makes for exotic and intriguing conjecture. These are names that have travelled from other places, sometimes thousands of miles away, to be transplanted in the Adirondacks. Sometimes quixotically romantic, sometimes heartbreakingly melancholic, our North Country has its "Mexico" as well as its "Klondike Brook." We have our "Norway," "Hague," "Santa Clara," "New Russia," "Vermontville" and even "Essex." These are "Transfer Names," and how they came to the Adirondacks makes for fascinating telling. But that's for a later chapter.

Let's stop for a minute and check to see if the whole family is with us. So far we've got "Foreign," "Personal," "Commemorative" and "Transfer." Our family is growing, and we can still recognize everyone.

Somewhat akin to the last family, "Transfer Names," are those which come to us from the Bible or from Greek or Roman antiquity. The Adirondacks are not remiss in our education, religious and classic; a number of names on the land attest to our love of the classics as well as the Bible, or at least a passing acquaintanceship with them!

We are blessed with a plurality of "Mt. Pisgahs;" we visit "Pharaoh Lake;" we climb our "Balm of Gilead Mountain;" we have our "Galilee," "Jericho" and "Jerusalem," not to speak of our "Sodom." Of the Greeks and Romans, we can find here in our Adirondacks the township of "Diana," "Ilion," "Mt. Etna," "Mt. Electra" and "Minerva."

By far the greatest number of names belong to their places and live there comfortably because they describe them accurately. They point at their place's size or shape or color or location or the plants that grow or the animals that visit or the climate that prevails. These "Descriptive Names" dot the landscape. And after all, as we shall see in the next chapter, that's really what most names are supposed to do: describe the place we're naming. But more on that later.

It is safe to say that you won't go anywhere in the Adirondacks without finding most of the names telling you something about the appearance or condition of the places. You'll find a "Long Lake" as well as a "Mirror Lake," a "Wolf Pond" and a "Mud Pond," a "North Branch" and a "South Meadow," a "Bear Mountain" and a "Beaver Brook," a "Lily Pond" and a "Cranberry Lake," a "Whiteface Mountain" and a hamlet called "Mountainview," a "Roaring Brook" and a "Salmon River," the hamlet of "Riverview" and the community of "Slab City." Sometimes conditions change, and the name describing its place seems less than accurate any more (at any rate, many people in "Lake Placid" would say so). But still it is a "descriptive" name, and because the place may change but not its name, we can learn about the past, as we will see.

One final group of names must be noted, partly because this category is so pleasurable in the seeing. These are fanciful or eccentric names (to us). Although their number is relatively small, their impact upon our imagination is deep and long-lasting. We know we are in the presence of a part of ourselves that delights in the absurd, that enjoys sticking the pin in the balloon of the pompous and respectably dull, that relishes seeing the look of dismay and embarrassment on the face of polite society.

When we come to a "Grog Harbor," a "Devil's Pulpit," a "Botheration Pond," a "Drunkard Creek," a "Grizzle Ocean Pond," a "Sober Kiln," a "Tight Nipping," a "Bum Pond," a "Poker Pond," a "Scuttle Hole Creek," an "Old Street," and of course, a "New Street," a "Moonshine Pond," a "Cream of the Valley Road," a "Hot Water Pond," a "Back Road," a "Lonesome Pond" and of course, our wonderful "Knowersville," we all feel somehow easier, somewhat more relaxed, as if we've come home from a formal dinner and slipped into more comfortable clothing. These fanciful and eccentric names give us a feel for the land and the people as nothing else can do.

So now we have all our categories, our kinds of names. Within these families of names all the places in the Adirondacks find their relatives and their homes. Having these categories does make our map-watching a bit easier and, I think, more enjoyable. Remember, to understand is to enjoy!

But I'm sure you've already seen the flaw in this system of categories. If this were the Ark built of all the families of names, there would be so many leaks we'd all be in deep water. The problem is in the categories. They overlap. A "Descriptive" name often has cousins or uncles among "Foreign" names. A "Biblical/Classical" name often feels very much at home with its sisters or grandparents among "Transfer" names. It is easier to number the angels on the head of a pin than to separate the families of names!

Fortunately, our system of families of names is not meant to keep us permanently or completely high and dry (even the Ark was grounded after forty days). No, our families of names do visit with each other and defy all attempts at exclusivity. Our names, then, in addition to all their other virtues, are profoundly democratic.

With that in mind, our scheme is useful in that we can handle more easily the Everest of Adirondack names. We can talk about our seven families: "Foreign," "Personal," "Commemorative," "Transfer," "Biblical/Classical," "Descriptive" and "Fanciful/Eccentric."

Now that we've met the family or families, let's see how names work. Let's take a look at what happens when a word gets used as a name. What happens to Tupper's lake when it becomes "Tupper Lake"?

3

There Is Nothing Like A Name

Well, we've seen thus far that sometimes it takes hundreds of years for a place to finally settle on its name, trying on one label after another, as at a fashion designer's salon, before deciding on the one exactly right. It certainly took our Adirondacks long enough—from around 1500 to about 1850—to decide. And we've also seen how many different kinds of names there are: personal ones and descriptive types; foreign names; those transferred from other places; commemorative as well as eccentric and fanciful; and surely our biblical and classical names.

Now let's take a look at what a name really is. After all, knowing what a thing is should help us understand how it works. First of all, a name is not a word. Or rather, names used to be words but became something else. Let's go back and see what happened.

In the beginning, there were only words. And words describe things, tell all about them: what they are made of, what they do, how they do it, when, where, why, to whom; in short, words tell us what things are. Words describe our worlds, and even, in the case of SciFi, words sometimes make up whole new worlds! There's a lot that can be said about the nature of words, and there's been mounds of books and mountains of words used to get at the nature and functions and history of words. What is important to us is that we see that words describe things.

Indeed, if you'll recall, one of the first things man did (if not the first) was to "word" things: that is, to give things a word, connecting that thing to that word. Once done, we could locate and identify and, in fact, recognize that thing. And since that thing now had a word, we could know that thing for what it is because its word describes it. Thus, for example, the word "turtle" creates for us and in us the thing itself, the turtle.

We know in reasonably general terms what this "word" turtle looks like, its shape and size; we know how it moves and its velocity; we know all about its shell and something about what it eats; we've picked up something about how long it lives. If we're really good about turtles, we've learned all kinds of things about them. So we can see, in this connection between the word "turtle" and the turtle itself, a world of recognition, of information, of identification. As Thoreau noted, nature does speak directly, whereas we speak through metaphors, through words.

Let's take another example, this time from another part of our world. Let's look at water, more particularly, "pond." In reasonably general terms we "know" ponds; the word gives us our images. We know a pond's color, its size, its shape; we know the plants and reeds and fish and birds and deer that live or visit the pond; in short, the word gives us our pond.

I know all this is pretty speculative, a bit "theoretical," but bear with me and we'll get back on solid ground pretty soon. Right now we have two words, "turtle" and "pond," each giving us lots of information and identification about their "things," the turtle and the pond. The funny thing is that my family and I used to live in Saranac Lake, and my home was on Turtle Pond! That is, not on the water itself, but all our mail came to Turtle Pond, the IRS pinpointed me on Turtle Pond, and my credit card bills came to Turtle Pond. I figure that if the mailman, the tax collector, and the Visa/Mastercard connection placed me on Turtle Pond, then Turtle Pond was where I lived.

Now we can see what begins to happen to words when they become names. I'm convinced that my postman and my tax and bill collectors did not first think of the clarity and color of water, the lilypads and bass, the muskrat and deer, the shell shape and age of the turtle, its sunning logs . . . no, they conjured up none of these images at first. For them, I am convinced, Turtle Pond had become no longer a combination of two words that described two things; Turtle Pond, for them and for most others, had become a name that locates a place.

Now sometimes when the press of "important" matters is not too great, when the world is not too much with us, sometimes someone says, "Are there turtles in the pond?," or, being pessimistic in this age, "Were there ever turtles?" I've always been delighted with this sort of question, for it reinforces my notions about words and names. What has happened is that for the moment, with that question, we have moved back to an earlier stage, when words were still words and described things.

Think back for a moment to our Adirondack names. Think how many names *meant* things, described things, identified things. Think of "Couchsachrage," "Avacal," even "Adirondack:" they all were words that had meaning, that told us about the thing, that were words before they became names.

Now, somewhere along the way, something very interesting happened. The purpose, the job, the function of the word changed. Somewhere along the path of human life the word as name became less and less geared to describe the thing, and more and more to identify it. So when you answer the "Where did you live?" with "On Turtle Pond," the interest is in establishing an identifiable place, not in describing a naturalistic environment. Indeed, most often the descriptive power declines and ultimately disappears, and what remains when a word evolves into a name is most often only the locating purpose.

For example, let's swing across the Adirondacks to the Fulton Chain, north and east of Utica. In the earliest of days after the Revolutionary War, woodsmen enjoyed the beauty and abundance of the lakes and mountains of this region. By the 1810s, Frederick Herreshoff was devoting his life and the remaining resources of his family to developing the area, opening up settlements, building roads, importing prize-winning sheep, and creating an iron ore industry replete with foundry. Herreshoff came to the Fulton Chain with the legacy of the John Brown family (again, not the Great Abolitionist of Harper's Ferry martyrdom) of Providence, Rhode Island, Revolutionary War fame. We'll hear more about him later, in connection with some wonderful Puritan virtues immortalized in Adirondack names.

Herreshoff himself is thought to have been an illegitimate son of a prominent member of the Prussian court. He enjoyed a classical education and was sent off to America to work in an import/export firm in New York City. By the turn of the century, Herreshoff had married one of the daughters of John Brown. Leaving New York, he and his wife settled in Providence, where Herreshoff became intimately involved in all the commercial activities of his father-in-law, including the China trade. Herreshoff's legacy to America, in addition to the Fulton Chain, rests in his illustrious offspring who became some of the most noted yacht designers in the United States. The Herreshoff name in East Coast boating is legendary.

Unfortunately for Herreshoff, his attempts to develop the Fulton Chain region failed. His roads attracted few permanent settlers, for more promising lands were available farther west; his prize sheep did withstand the winter months but fell victim to bands of wolves; his fields proved more hospitable to foraging forest animals than to cultivating crops. Indeed, even today the Fulton Chain boasts a sparse population and an abundance of wild-life.

Herreshoff witnessed the failures of his attempts to develop the region. His final hopes rested upon ore tracings unearthed near the middle branch of the Moose River. Herreshoff directed the excavation of a mine at a place now known as "Thendara," and he had a forge built close by. Things seemed, finally, to be going his way, but it was not to be.

On a Sunday morning in December of 1819, two years after the ore mine had begun producing, Herreshoff's foreman, the story now goes, came to the manor house and reported that the main shaft of the mine had flooded. In those days, serious flooding marked the end of any operations because equipment had not been devised to deal with the immense amounts of water involved in a mine flooding. Herreshoff is said to have thanked his foreman, sent him on his way, locked himself in his study . . . and put a revolver to his head. This calamity saw the end of any attempt to settle the region for a number of decades.

The mine entrance is still available to the knowing and observable eye, however hidden by soil and grasses. The forge, of course, lay silent and rusting, a monument to human hopes and an emblematic witness to personal tragedy. The area seemed to revert to its earlier, natural state, and the occasional woodsman marked the forge as he moved between the comforts of civilized Utica and the grandeur of the untouched lakes and mountains and forests of the wilds of the Brown's Tract.

These occasional travelers began to refer to the remains of Herreschoff's last attempt to develop the area as "The Forge." They began to see it as a distance marker, a reference point between the heart of the forest and civilization. They began to relate incidents in terms of the area of the deserted forge. "Stopped two days ago at the forge," they might be overheard to report casually to a friend. They began to give directions, such as "When you get to the forge, you've only got three more days to reach. . . ." Or they might begin a story of hunting with, "Saw the biggest moose tracks you ever did see right down from the forge."

Before long, the phrase "the forge" acquired a familiarity, a kind of comfortable domesticity that ironically belied its abandoned condition. Instead of "the forge," our woodsmen began to speak of "the old forge." And now you've surely got it, if you've ever been down around the Fulton Chain. Gradually (and naturally, for this is the way of things as we use our language), "the old forge" ultimately, inexorably dropped its generalizing "the" and became a bona fide, a proper, place name, "Old Forge."

So we have seen how one of the most exciting and attractive places in the Adirondacks took its name from a word, "forge." The phrase became a locator, a referent; i.e., the point from Utica into the wilds where an abandoned forge remained. And finally, as we use descriptive words in the service of naming things, the old forge became "Old Forge."

I can't help sharing another example with you. Not because you haven't gotten the point yet, but merely because the name we're going to look at is so interesting. We'll see an absolute shift from descriptive power to locator power and the complete loss of understanding of the "meaning" of the name when it evolved from description to location.

Let's drive up the Northway from Albany as we head into the Adirondacks past Lake George and along Lake Champlain. One of the first major communities we come to along Lake Champlain is "Ticonderoga," pronounced by all of us who live in the North Country as "Ti," that is, the same as that which one does with ropes (I've told you about "Pru" for "Peru" and "Ti" for "Ticonderoga" so you'll be comfortable talking with us as you tour through the Adirondacks).

The fort and the settlement sit at a crucial point. It is the opening of the major waterway, Lake Champlain, the doorway to Canada, and, via the St. Lawrence River, to Europe. Its strategic position overlooks the waters that feed into and are the beginnings of Lake Champlain. This made it a vital site to Mohawk, Algonkian, French, English and, finally, American interests, first from a military point of view, then from commercial and trade sensibilities. No nation or people felt that they were safe in the North Country until they controlled the point at what we call "Ti."

The Mohawk called the place "CHI-GON-DER-O-GA," that is, "the place where waters sing as they swiftly cascade over the rocks into the lake." A nicely poetic and certainly closely descriptive indication of the physical quality of the place. Now the Mohawk did not ever say "Ticonderoga;" they most likely never even said "CHI-GON-DER-O-GA." We really don't know how they pronounced this descriptive word. It probably didn't mean exactly what that poetic phrase says, either! But it probably meant something like that.

What comes to us is a hint at Mohawk pronunciation and Mohawk meaning, recorded by travelers and explorers who tried to recreate, on paper, the sounds they heard of a language very foreign to their ears. What they were able to give us was a very suspect approximation of what they thought they heard.

It reminds me of Mark Twain's line about *The Deerslayer*'s Natty Bumppo, the hero of James Fenimore Cooper's Leather-stocking novels. Natty roamed the lower Adirondacks; in fact, we believe that a Revolutionary War veteran, Nat Foster, who hunted and lived in the Fulton Chain (we're back there again) was the woodsman known to the young Cooper and the model of our woodsman hero. Cooper gave Natty an Indian companion, just as the radio script writers did over a hundred years later when the Lone Ranger had his Tonto. Natty's sidekick was Chingachgook, as faithful to the Deerslayer as ever Tonto was to the Masked Man. Mark Twain wrote, and I'm sure with enormous pleasure, that he found it difficult pronouncing this faithful companion's name, that the name was part of Cooper's many literary offenses, and that he would, for the remainder of his (Twain's) essay (and I suspect his life as well) call Natty's companion "Chicago."

So it is that we try to recreate the sounds of the word used by the Mohawk to describe this place on the southern edge of Lake Champlain. We end up reading on our maps and saying "Ticonderoga" (or "Ti"). Its meaning—"the place where waters sing as they swiftly cascade over the rocks into the lake"—has become quite irrelevant, for we are concerned almost exclusively with the need to locate the place, not describe it.

One final illustration. We've looked at an English name, "Old Forge," and an American Indian name, "Ticonderoga." Let's take a trip to the Raquette Lake and River country west of Blue Mountain Lake. We're not in a village now; we're on water, and "Raquette" is a funny way to spell an American name.

Well, of course, "Raquette" is French, not English, but some say it used to describe the awful noise of the rushing waters as the spring snows melt. A more dramatic form of "Ticonderoga," you might say. So "Raquette" means a loud din, a racket. Perhaps. But let's take another look and another trip—this time in years, not miles—and go back to the agitation and turmoil of the time just before the Revolutionary War broke out.

At a place called Fish House, just outside Saratoga on a main road from Albany, there lived—or tried to live—Sir John Johnson, the only recognized son of Sir William Johnson. Sir William had been the most successful Indian agent England was to enjoy, and a very powerful figure among the English colonists and among many of the Mohawk nation. Sir William had loved and lived with Molly Brant, sister of the War Chief Joseph, daughter of Mohawk aristocracy, and mother of quite a number of sons by Sir William. This lineage and history had, of course, no bearing in terms of English law and social convention. Sir John was the only rightful heir of the recently deceased Sir William.

Sir William, by the way, is credited with winning over the affection, and therefore loyalty, of many of the Iroquois in the Crown's battle with the French for control of this part of the New World. Indeed, Johnson was knighted when he was able to rally enough Mohawk support under Joseph Brant to defeat the

French at "La Lac du Sacrement," which Johnson promptly rechristened "George" in honor of his King.

It may be that Johnson was knighted as much for naming Lake George as he was for the military victory, given the state of court politics in London at that time. We have no way of measuring the power of a name! Whatever the case, William had become Sir William and a vital factor in England's successes. His son, John, inherited his title, despite William's partiality and love for Molly and his children by her. Those children all suffered the tortured lives of the no-man's land of "half-breed" and "white-eyes" ostracism as John came into the title and the possessions of his father.

Sir John Johnson, then, enjoyed the power, wealth and prestige of the most important agent of the Crown in the northern part of the colony. And he maintained an intense degree of loyalty to the Crown in the face of the agitation and dissent which kept building up more and more in the early 1770s.

With the issue coming to a head, Tories in the Albany area lined themselves with Sir John as they faced the growing rancor of the rebels, and Albany, like almost all other cities, witnessed violence and property destruction when supporters of the king were driven from their homes by insurgents. And so, the story goes, Sir John and a group of loyalists raided the already confiscated Johnson Hall, dug up some silver buried under floor boards, and fled into the forests of the "Antient Couchsachrage" to escape the rebels and join forces with other loyalists north of the St. Lawrence River.

They worked their way north through the winter forests, using snowshoes to traverse the snow-covered landscape. Legend has it that a cannon (uncovered in our time, submerged in a pond) was abandoned by Sir John's party as they struggled through the woods. Another legend insists that at one point, hungry and desperate, they were rescued by a band of loyalists who had come down from Canada to find and save Sir John and his followers. The leader of this rescue mission is reported to have been Captain Peter Sabattis, a Native American war chief whose son became a famous guide in the early part of the nineteenth century and after whom the settlement of "Sabattis" is named.

But, after the sinking of the cannon—if that story is true—
and before being rescued by Captain Sabattis—if that story is
also true—between these "perhapses" Sir John's band supposedly came to a major waterway just at the time when the ice was
breaking up and the snows melting, the signs of Adirondack
springtime. Snowshoes, therefore, were no longer of any use. The
story continues with a mountain of snowshoes deposited upon
the shore of a large lake, and canoes taking their place.

And the lake and waterway took the name "Raquette,"
after the French term for "snowshoe." True? Perhaps. Perhaps
not. But the story is worth telling.

What is not questionable is that we have a name,
"Raquette," which hints at its meaning through the stories told
about it. But whatever the truth of those clues, the main purpose
for most of us in the name "Raquette" is in its power to tell us
what place it is and where it is. The name may be Native
American or French or English, it may be a village, a fort, a lake,
a river: what counts is that the word for that place has become
the name for that place. The meaning of the word is now
irrelevant to its main use.

This is why I say that names are unique. They began as
words, they look like words; sometimes, as we'll see, they go back
to being words, but when they are names they are something
else.

When we can see through something, we often call it
translucent; when we can't, we often call it opaque. So when a
word loses its meaning in becoming a name, it also loses its
translucent quality and becomes opaque. This analogy, helping
us see how names differ from words, has been made popular and
useful through the efforts of Professor Wilhelm Nicolaisen, an
internationally noted linguist and name scholar currently
teaching at the State University of New York at Binghamton.

We are now ready for our First Law of Names (clearer but
not as amusing as First Name Law) which we should label, in
honor of the Sir John story, "The Racket." These "laws," by the
way, have been formulated entirely for your amusement; most if
not all name scholars would not elect them.

The First Name Law, alias The Racket: The degree of
translucence of a name is in inverse proportion to its age: the
older the name, the greater its tendency toward opaqueness.

Sometimes names carry with them built-in translators, so that you can move them from the opaque to the translucent. Generally we do this only after we've used the name as a name and then become curious as to its meaning, as with "Turtle Pond." So, for example, we can easily translate "AuSable Forks Village," and make out that the branches of the river with this French name meet here and became the site of a settlement, the French "AuSable" meaning "at the sand." Same principle with Plattsburgh. But unless you know Anglo-Saxon, "Essex" is merely a county as well as a village; you wouldn't know "Essex" as "the easternmost part." We do work out "Ausable," but what about "Saranac?"

Along with losing their descriptive role—or rather *because* they lose their descriptive role—names often lose their ability to create emotional responses. When the place upon which Syracuse sits was first named by Native Americans, it was known as "Stink Hole." The locals had taken note of the salt swamps and the emerging miasma, and a realistic—not classic Roman—name rose.

Now "Stink Hole" says something, and we react to it; you might say the name seals the place's fate! But unless you are a classicist, "Syracuse" carries with it very little except to locate which city you are approaching from the Thruway. You'd be surprised at how many names of places have older word-meanings that would shock you! But that's for another book.

Back at this book, we're ready for our Second Name Law. This time we'll call it, in honor of Syracuse, "The Stink Hole."

The Second Name Law, alias The Stink Hole: the greater the degree of opaqueness, the greater the loss of emotional response.

There is one exception to the Second Name Law. Sometimes a name picks up an emotional charge because of events or myths about its place. Then things get reversed and the place gives its name emotions. For example, to say you were "Pearl Harbored" suggests a devastating surprise attack. Almost like meeting your own "Waterloo." Enough of this! Let's concentrate on happy things like finding your own "Shangri-La." I haven't found many places in the Adirondacks whose names carry this kind of happy emotional charge, not even one

"Golden Pond." If you find one, let me know for the next edition of this book.

It would be convenient were we able to leave it at First and Second Name Laws, but there are two more we must be introduced to. Say hello to "The Domestic."

Have you ever looked at a map, and noticed an area without any names on it? Or very few? Such as some older maps of the Arctic and Antarctic regions. Sure you have, and you know what that means. People don't live there. Or very few. When you find a place that never had any people, you find a place with no names. The land is nameless, uninhabited. If you find a place with names but no people, you know that there were people there at some time in the past. As we say, "Show me a place with lots of names and I'll show you a place with lots of people." In short, names are the markers indicating human presence.

The name lifts the place out from the unmarked landscape and gives it a kind of "human permanence." The name makes that place unique in that from the time of its naming the place is separated out and is different from all other places. But at the same time, the name settles the place, gives it familiarity, and makes it known and no longer foreign. In short, names domesticate.

As in the beginning, there was the word; just so, in the beginning of civilization, there was the name. Now we can formulate our Third (I wish we could call it the "Middle") Name Law, the one that made the world livable.

The Third Name Law, alias The Domestic: Show me place names and I'll show you human presence.

This brings us to the last of the "Four Laws of Names," "Digs." Names are like pieces of ancient pottery, fragments of dinosaur bone, bits of pre-historic furniture. Times change, civilizations move on, land masses shift, settlements become buried beneath newer peoples; nevertheless, the record of what did go on can often be traced and described through the artifacts left behind in the archaeological sites. Called "digs," these are the archaeologists' source of material enabling them to reconstruct earlier civilizations as well as earlier forms of life.

Just so, names very often stay on the land long after the people who gave them are gone. And since the name was at first a descriptive word, it often offers hints as to what kind of rocks or plants or water or animals were there. The name may also offer hints as to the people themselves, in that the way they named a place is a clue to the way they saw the world, the parts of the world important to them.

Now we're ready for our next name law, which we can nickname, "digs."

The Fourth Name Law, alias Digs: Names are as good as sticks and bones for knowing the past.

So we now have four laws to help us understand what names are and how they work.

- The Racket: as words become names they become more opaque.
- The Stink Hole: as names become opaque they lose their emotional charge.
- The Domestic: as with love and marriage, humans and names go together.
- Digs: names are languages' dinosaur bones.

Armed with these four laws, we can now really begin to look at what names in the Adirondacks tell us about the people who came here and the place they came to.

4

The Rorschäch Test

It all began on a cold and wintry day near the tail end of a cold and seemingly endless wintry winter: days upon days of frigid winds, snow drifts of five to ten feet permanently attached to the ground, heavy dark clouds. (It really wasn't all that bleak, merely a vision colored by my yen for summer, and I was seeing just what I wanted to see). I was at my desk, poring over maps when I spied a puzzling repetition of a name on an old map covering the Keene Valley, Lake Placid, Saranac Lake area: I noticed two instances of "Mt. Pisgah."

I thought, "Sure, according to the Old Testament Mt. Pisgah was the place from where Moses saw the Promised Land. But two Mt. Pisgahs seems a bit much, especially on a day like this." I called to my wife, sarcasm dripping with each word: "These people must have come from places worse than Hell to call this the Promised Land. The Mohawk knew better. They were smart enough not to live here all year round." You see, people in the Adirondacks know that our year has only two seasons: Summer Black Fly and Winter Snow Fly.

Then I went back to my search for any clues that the names on the maps could give me about the people who gave those names. And then, of course, it hit me! "Mt. Pisgah" offers us as much information, if of a different kind, as any other name, even the most clearly descriptive.

I had, till that moment, gone by the common assumption that there is always an objective and verifiable connection between a name and its place, something measurable. The common assumption is that if we dig deep enough into geological strata, or past events, or linguistic forms, we'll find *something* about the place. Something measurably physical, or documentably historic, or phonetically and/or etymologically linguistic. *Something* that will explain the connection between the name and the place. The assumption is that objectively verifiable connections always exist.

For example, "Pleasant Valley" appears fully accessible to us as a descriptive phrase; that is, as a word, as well as a name. Nothing opaque about this name. We know how it came to be because as a word it is completely understandable. "Cobble Hill" is a bit less so, because many of us (including myself) need reminding that a "cobble" is not only a smallish stone but also a small hill, as in "hillock." So it may be that we are unknowingly saying "Hill Hill" when we say "Cobble Hill," just as we say "River Big River" when we refer to the "Rio Grande River." "Cobble" is more opaque than "Pleasant." And, as we've noted previously, a name such as "Essex County" has become fully opaque. Not many of us think of the name as telling us that this is the place most to the east, the "easternmost part." No, "Essex County" means a place, not a direction.

We almost always try to see why and how a place took its name by understanding the lay of the land. And rightly so, given that names began as words that describe. However, there is another landscape to be explored, thanks to our "Mt. Pisgahs." Sometimes the name tells us as much about the character and background and hopes of the people giving the name as about the place itself.

Just think about "Mt. Pisgah" for a moment. Can we not see in our mind's eye God-fearing, Bible-reading Yankees traversing the mountains and after a great deal of hardship coming to a vista, a view looking down onto a hospitable valley in which they could end their wanderings and settle peacefully into clearing the land and enjoying the fruits of their labor and God's bounty? Surely a romantic notion, but does not the name "Mt. Pisgah"—and two of them—suggest that some of the people who came to this part of the Adirondacks perceived their world in such a way? And doesn't that hint at their way of life, their values and practices, and therefore one part of the life of the entire region? Names really are a Rorschäch Test; they hint at things about the namers.

Well, names given by honest settlers are one thing, you might say, and maybe do hint at their hopes and beliefs, but what about other kinds of names? Let's look at Franklin County's seat of government, "Malone."

"Malone" was separated from "Chateaugay" in 1805 and both the township and the settlement were called "Harison." It seems one of the members of the Macomb syndicate was a Mr. Richard Harison. The Macomb group, by the way, were a prize lot whose land operations were on a scale so large that contemporary land speculators seem small potatoes by comparison. The Macomb Syndicate got hold of four million acres (more or less) for a mere ten thousand dollars! More about them later.

Maybe to avoid unnecessary publicity, maybe for personal reasons, whatever prompted it, in 1808, three years later, "Harison" became "Ezraville." It so happens that Mr. Richard Harison enjoyed a close friendship with a Long Island resident, Mr. Ezra L'Hommedieu. Four years after that, Harison once again changed the name of the township and village. Perhaps he decided that "Ezraville" had a grating sound, not smooth enough; perhaps there was a falling out amongst friends. Whatever prompted it, in 1812, "Ezraville" became "Malone." Another friend of Mr. Harison was to be immortalized, a Mr. Edmond Malone.

For those of you who have experienced the joys and agonies of "University Graduate Degree Programs in English Literature," or know of a friend or loved one exposed to such a fate, the name Edmond Malone might ring a bell. He was the pre-eminent Shakespearean scholar and critic of his time on both sides of the Atlantic (some two hundred years later, his reputation is just as bright).

Whatever we might think about Harison and the Macomb Purchase speculators, we must admit that to name a place in honor of a friend who happens to be that age's most famous Shakespearean expert indicates a breadth of experiences and sensibilities and social contacts beyond that which we think of as part of a real estate speculator's world. *Wall Street Journal* perhaps; Elizabethan Theater, never.

We can also assume that most of the settlers in "Malone" had never heard of Edmond Malone. The name was imposed

from the top—which can be the way with names not descriptive
of the land.

If the farmers of the "Mt. Pisgahs" carried their Bibles and
were motivated in part by religious sensibilities, we can
speculate that the proprietors of "Malone" carried their Classics
and were motivated in part by literary and aesthetic sensibilities.
The point, of course, is that these names describe the psychic
geography of the namers rather than the physical geography of
the land.

By the way, if you ever have occasion to look at some older
maps, or see tax lists of properties in local newspapers, or
purchase some property in the Adirondacks, you will more than
likely run across the phrase "Macomb's Purchase" or "Great
Tract No. 1" (right up to No. 6). It is this land development
scheme that Harison had connections with. And it is a
remarkable story.

It begins with Alexander Macomb, an adventurer who after
the French and Indian War and, indeed, through the Revolutionary and Post-Revolutionary War years, roamed extensively
throughout the northern frontier. He was quite familiar with the
St. Lawrence Valley, the Great Lakes, the Lower Canada region,
and our "Antient Couchsachrage." His business was complex
and international: he had intimate contacts with French as well
as English aristocracy. In fact, his first wife, an illegitimate
daughter of Henry IV, King of France, died, and Macomb
ultimately remarried into the Dutch patroon family the
Livingstons.

Whatever his activities with his French connections before
1760 and his English connections between the end of the French
and English fighting and the beginning of the English and
American fighting, by the conclusion of the Revolutionary War
Macomb was a well-known and respected figure among wealthy
"American" circles. His connection with the Livingston family
gave him the contacts; his unique knowledge of the features and
extent of the "Antient Couchsachrage" at a time when very few
people knew anything about the area made him a valued figure
and consultant. And at a time when Indian land claims were
being dismissed or settled in order to pave the way for serious
land speculation and development, Alexander Macomb became
a man much in demand.

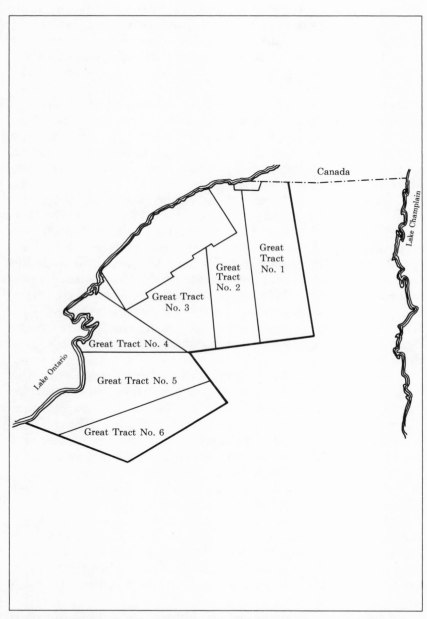

Map of Macomb's Purchase with the six tracts outlined.

He became involved with two wealthy speculators from New York City (how contemporary it sounds), and in January of 1792 a deed for four million acres (more or less, of course) was turned over to Macomb by the state of New York in consideration of which the state received the sum of ten thousand dollars—some 1/4 penny per acre (more or less). Indeed, there was a hue and cry in Albany, and charges or whispers of "influence." But nothing was ever proved. The deed was described as comprising six tracts, and since the purchase covered so much of the Adirondacks, a great many of our present ownership and tax documents refer to the specific tract and title, Macomb Purchase (see page 51).

One of the two New York City men behind Macomb was Daniel McCormick, a native of Ireland who had come to the New World as a young boy and had made his way into Wall Street, amassing a fortune in trade during the Revolutionary War. The stories about McCormick, besides his great wealth, include his habits of dress. It seems that as late as the 1840s when he was quite an old man, McCormick would walk down Wall Street from his home to his offices dressed in the fashion of the 1770s! He must have caused a sensation, looking like pictures of George Washington in his stockinged britches, jacket with tails, and three-cornered hat.

Those who care for the writings of Herman Melville, the Dutch schoolteacher from the Albany area, will also be interested in McCormick, if only as a footnote. Melville wrote not only about Ishmael, Captain Ahab and Moby Dick. There were different leviathans he hunted, and I think one of them did swim in the commercial oceans. Melville's visionary short story "Bartleby The Scrivener" is said to rely upon Daniel McCormick as the model for the "Employer" in the Wall Street office where the story takes place.

His colorful dress and background notwithstanding, McCormick played a minor role in the history of the Macomb Purchase. His financial investment was considerable, of course, but he allowed a younger, fellow Wall Street financier to carry most of the burdens of the development and selling off of the land.

Such was William Constable. In January, 1792 Macomb receives the deed for the four million acres from the State of New

York; six months later, in June of 1792, the deed for the entire purchase, all six tracts, is in the hands of McCormick and Constable. Alexander Macomb vanishes from our story in the Adirondacks.

But as a postscript on Macomb, he ends up in New York City linked with Alexander Hamilton in a scheme to create a water supply system for the city. The scheme goes bankrupt, and Macomb ends in debtor's prison. Such is the Wheel of Fortune! But if you drive from Manhattan's uptown west side into the Bronx, towards Yankee Stadium, you will, if having my luck, find yourself inching across a bridge in a traffic jam. This is an historical blessing in disguise because at the apex of the bridge you will see a metal plaque commemorating the force behind the bridge and the aqueduct (despite debtor's prison): Mr. Alexander Macomb!

But back to June, 1792. Macomb is out, Constable and McCormick in. July of that same year finds Constable sitting in the salons of Parisian aristocracy . . . selling real estate. The frightened nobility are feeling the presence of the revolutionaries sharpening the guillotine; heads are beginning to fall; the Bastille is being liberated. According to Charles Dickens, Madame DeFarge, of the *Tale of Two Cities,* is deep into her knitting; "Let Them Eat Cake" has turned rancid.

And here is William Constable selling real estate! And being quite successful. A consortium emerges, calling itself "La Compagnie de New York," and underwritten by French aristocracy. The "Compagnie" purchases all of Tract No. 5, and develops plans to survey the area and establish another "New France" in the Adirondacks. Constable and McCormick are paid more for Tract No. 5 than they paid for the entire Macomb Purchase!

The French called their new possession "Castorland," after the French word for "beaver," and despite the ultimate failure of this second French invasion of the Adirondacks, the name "Castor" remained with us in the form of a station on the New York Central Railroad's St. Lawrence line. The story of the Castorland experiment is a fascinating one and worth your looking at in Edith Pilcher's fine study, *Castorland.*

But let us leave these side rails and get back to our story about names. From "Pisgah" to "Malone" and then sidetracked

to the Macomb Purchase and "Castorland," we now come to
another place whose names tell us a lot about the namers. Let's
stop off at the seat of Essex County: Elizabethtown, known to all
of us as "E'town."

Elizabeth was the wife of William, or Will, for whom
Willsboro is named. Or rather, from whom Willsboro got its
name. You see, William Gilliland named Elizabethtown in
honor of his wife, and he named Willsboro in honor of himself.
This is one of only two husband-and-wife teams I know of whose
names continue together this way in the Adirondacks; it is also
the only instance I know of in which the honors were so self-
awarded! Ironically enough, William named the more important
community after himself, but time has made Elizabeth the
winner, since "Elizabeth's town" is the county seat and "Will's
boro" has declined in importance.

Three additional communities in this part of the Adirondacks, in and near Essex County, bore the names of members of
William's family. I believe such a gathering of the clan
(Elizabeth, Will, Bess, Charlotte and James) deserves having its
story told.

It seems that at an earlier time, only four years after the
French were removed from the Adirondacks, about 1764,
William came up from New York City where, like McCormick
and Constable about thirty years later (and a whole string of
similar types right up to today), Gilliland had made a great deal
of money. Also like McCormick, Gilliland came from a poor Irish
background and arrived in New York City in 1758, with an
honorable discharge from the British Army.

He worked hard and married well, and the combination of
diligence, luck and intelligence brought him a fortune in
financial successes on Wall Street. I suspect his early years and
the impressions of English estates dotting the Irish landscapes of
his earliest days never left Gilliland's memory, for he devoted
the remainder of his life—and his considerable fortune—to
attempting to recreate the baronial life he had seen, if only from
a distance and perhaps in imagination, in his native Ireland. I
suspect as well that his awareness of the magnificent estates
created by the Dutch aristocracy in the lower and central
Hudson valley kept his ambitions close to mind.

The great estates of the Dutch families—the Cortlands,

Livingstons, Rensselaers, Schuylers—embraced almost all the Hudson Valley and the Albany area. Thus Gilliland was forced to look farther afield. And so it was that in 1764 Gilliland purchased large tracts of land in the newly won "Antient Couchsachrage," north of Albany—indeed, north of Lake George. His purchases tended to coincide with the surveyed boundaries of the French estates that had been created during the century (more or less) of French influence along both sides of Lake Champlain. Just keep an eye out for older buildings and you'll catch an occasional glimpse of French architecture. Just look sharply along the roadside and you'll see vines, the vestiges of earlier vineyards. Just check your maps and you'll see all the places with French names!

Gilliland's resources allowed him to become the benefactor of English military supremacy over the French, at least initially. He purchased one tract of some 3,500 acres embracing the mouth of that which is called the Bouquet River, now known as Westport. There was another tract of 4,500 acres nearby which he named after his daughter, using the familiar of Elizabeth, Bess. Another settlement on the Salmon River he called after his brother, James. At the edge of Plattsburgh, on Cumberland Head, was another settlement purchased by Gilliland and called after another daughter, Charlotte. These are in addition to the settlements he named after his wife and himself. So the early maps and records note the existence of Bessboro, Jamesboro, Charlottesboro, Willsboro and, of course, Elizabethtown.

All this buying of land and family naming! Unfortunately, the cost proved very high for Gilliland. In the process of moving up to his new lands, Gilliland's infant daughter was lost when a raft overturned in a rapid between Lake George and Lake Champlain. And her death was just the start, as we shall see.

Gilliland brought numerous people up from New York City and other places to help create his dream of a baronial estate. Craftsmen such as blacksmiths and farriers, stonemasons and carpenters, as well as farmers, were induced to come to the new lands. Gilliland brought to his tracts the pioneers who would carve his manor out of the wilderness. And for twelve years Gilliland supervised the growth of his estates as a gentleman "squire," one of "landed gentry" pretensions, in the manner of those back in Ireland. He was the final judge and jury as well as law-giver; he was the provider of goods as well as store-keeper; he was the designer of all policy, economic and political and social. His brother, James, was the bailiff, the chief administrative officer. They farmed and hunted and cleared the land and built grist mills and lumber mills and roads and homes.

After twelve years of hard work and impressive results, Gilliland found himself in the midst of the upheaval of the Revolutionary War. His estates lay directly in the path of one of the most important military routes in the Northeast: the waterway that separates New England from the rest of the colonies and from Lower Canada: that is, the St. Lawrence River, Lake Champlain, Lake George and the Hudson River.

Gilliland's estates (see page 57) were the grounds upon which English and Colonial troops moved back and forth as the war progressed from one stage to another. And since Gilliland was of Irish background, with the soul of a rebel and adventurer, he sided with the revolutionaries and gave of his land and his wealth. At one point, Gilliland housed and fed through a winter season an entire regiment of "American" soldiers. And he helped them fell trees and use his iron deposits and foundry in the building of a flotilla, for these were the troops under the command of Benedict Arnold, a hero at the naval battle on Lake Champlain at Valcour Island, long before his name became coupled with treachery.

Of course, the British knew of Gilliland's efforts. They retaliated when the rebel forces ebbed south to the Lake George and Albany area. The British burned out almost all the settlements in Gilliland's tracts. If that sounds like modern guerrilla warfare, you can be assured that contemporary guerrilla strategy is not especially different from that of 200–some-odd years ago.

By the end of the Revolutionary War, Gilliland had suffered such enormous losses that, despite his strong sense that the cause of freedom was priceless, he was induced by his family and friends to apply to the Continental Congress for compensation for his losses. Unfortunately, there was little the Continental Congress could do, for it had almost no resources and innumerable requests. Gilliland received a commemorative plaque from the Congress, thanking him in the name of the

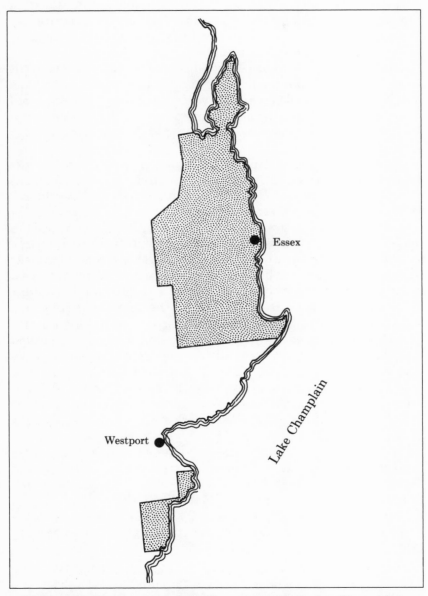

Gilliland's estates (partial schematic) on Lake Champlain.

people of the freed states and in the name of the spirit of Freedom. But he received not a penny. Gilliland was reduced by the burdens of enormous debts and forced into—of all things— New York City's debtor prison!

He was ultimately rescued by his son-in-law, and ended his days in the Adirondacks. The story is that he wandered off in the woods on a winter's day while surveying a parcel of one of his old tracts now owned by a development company. He was found the following spring—frozen to death on his dream of a baronial estate.

What remains of Gilliland's legacy is the vision of the attempt to impress one's life on the land. The Adirondacks sloughed off "Jamesboro" and "Charlottesboro" and "Bessboro." What remains of this remarkable man and his family and his attempts to create a world on the Adirondack landscape are the names of him and his wife, "Willsboro" and "Elizabethtown."

When you drive into the High Peaks area of the Adirondacks or locate on a map our highest elevation in New York, you see a name that we know is commemorative. The name for our tallest place in New York was bestowed by others to honor someone. We're not talking about "Twin Towers;" we're looking up at a beautiful and awe-inspiring mountain, said to have been called "Tahawus" or "the cloud-splitter" by some Iroquois, from "twawston," "to pierce." The authority for this derivation remains an early and romantically inclined journalist. What is incontrovertible is that this highest place in New York State is Mt. Marcy, named after New York's Governor William L. Marcy.

"Mt. Marcy" comes from the same source, in more ways than one, as does "Adirondacks," for it was that professor of chemistry at Williams College and New York state geologist, Ebenezer Emmons, who gave us "Marcy" as well as "Adirondack." He wrote in Assembly Document 200, p. 241, referring to his climb to the peak of this highest elevation in the state in August, 1837:

> . . . it is not surprising that names have not been given to the highest points of land in the state. This privilege belongs by common consent to the first explorers. This, to be sure, is but of little consequence; still, as things must have a name, the party saw fit to confer upon a few of the highest summits

designations by which they may in future be known. As this tour of exploration was made by gentlemen who were in the discharge of their duties to the state, and under the direction of the present executive, whose interest in the survey has been expressed both by public recommendations and private counsel and advice, it was thought that a more appropriate name could not be conferred on the highest summit of this group than Mount Marcy.

Emmons's words illustrate perfectly the notion that commemorative and personal names tell us about the times and the personages that were instrumental in shaping the events of the day.

We are now ready for the Fifth Name Law, which we will call, in honor of Emmons, Marcy's Mantle.

The Fifth Name Law, alias Marcy's Mantle: Show me a commemorative name and I'll show you who or what was important to the namers and their times.

Consider this law in the light of "Lake Flower," in Saranac Lake village. As we shall see in the next few pages (more or less), this body of water received its name from the then governor, not from its plant life. Governor Flower was indeed a crucial link in the creation of this lake. The Fifth Name Law does seem to work.

Let's go back further in time and move away from our map just a little, so that we can scan the entire Adirondack country. Let's go back to the excitement of the new country and its heroes, to the excitement of new lands and new worlds to conquer, back to the Adirondacks of 1790 to 1820. In those thirty years (more or less), most of the counties in the Adirondacks were carved out of the wilderness and granted political and legal status. Now, although they were not physical entities such as mountains and rivers, they too, as Emmons would note, needed to be named. And they were.

Washington County, Franklin County, Jefferson County, Hamilton County, Clinton County—these attest, of course, to the patriotic fervor which pervaded life throughout the early years of America's birth. And Fulton County commemorates its favorite adopted son, Robert Fulton. You can use these county names as a beginning primer for a course in American history! And rightly so, because these names of our Adirondack counties

reflect our admiration and reverence for the symbols of the
national will that created our country. In short, these are our
first heroes, and we commemorate their names on our land. Yes,
the Fifth Name Law works.

Another category of names also tells us about the people
who used them. Transfer names, in fact, often tell us more about
the namers than about the place itself. When we see in the North
Country places like "Hague," "New Sweden," "Norway," "New
Russia," "Santa Clara," "Mexico," "Madrid," we can be sure
they hint at those places back in someone's "old country," or in
someone's romantic psyche.

Even good old English names get transferred from a
previous home, sometimes more than once. "Essex" comes to us
from neighboring Vermont, as does the obvious "Vermontville."
However, "Essex" came from Vermont after moving from
Massachusetts after leaving England. "Bangor" moves to the
Adirondacks from New, not Old England. "Milton" in Saratoga
County left many relatives on the east side of Lake Champlain.

Often a transfer name reflects a sense of melancholy, a sense
of longing for the place from which one came, an attempt to take
along to the new home as much of the old as possible. Sometimes
there is something about the new home, like harsh winters, that
conjures up and fathers the new name: "New Russia."
Sometimes a peculiarity, like very fine iron ore, gives rise to the
name: "Dannemora."

Whatever the motive—wishing for the past, or bringing the
past to the present, or remembering one's background, or being
reminded of the past by something in the new, or wishing for the
exotic—whatever the reason, transfer names tell us profoundly
sensitive things about the people who came and settled the
land.

Well, we've seen some Biblical names, some personal
names, some commemorative names and some transfer names.
And we've seen how they often can help us know more about the
early days and the early people. There is one more type of name
that can tell us about those who made those names. Often we run
across names that seem funny to our ear, or old-fashioned, or
outrageous. In short, eccentric names. And as we smile or laugh
at the names, let's remember that they often tell us more about
the namer than do mounds of documents.

We'll go back to the Fulton ˙Chain for some very special names. Robert Fulton, by the way, had been hired by New York State as an expert on canal transportation after he had returned from Europe, where he had studied canals used in the Netherlands and France and Germany. This was the period when canals were the wave of the future: remember, the Erie Canal was open by 1825–26.

Fulton spent months exploring just that area Herreschoff had tried to develop. He acknowledged the potential of the sequence of lakes, rivers and canals from Tupper Lake to the Mohawk River, and he saw how the lakes in the Brown's Tract made the southern end of the scheme possible. But he came to the reluctant conclusion that, notwithstanding the beauties of the lakes and streams in "Brown's Tract," the difficulty of linking the lakes with operable canals and lifts was too great to allow for a feasible plan. Perhaps because of his flowing description of the beauties of the area, perhaps because his report meant the land would remain in its reasonably pristine state, the sequence of lakes became known as "The Fulton Chain."

But some thirty years before Robert Fulton and some ten years before Herreshoff, another man had traversed some of these lakes attempting to determine their potential. He was the unwitting purchaser of this tract of wild, newly available real estate, our John Brown of Providence, Rhode Island.

There is, of course, *the John Brown* and his grave on his farm in North Elba, just outside Lake Placid. And we'll get to him a bit later in connection with our own "Timbuktu." We're going to talk about the Rhode Island John Brown now, the John Brown for whom the "Brown's Tract" had been named. Here is the oft-repeated story, although a new book, *John Brown's Tract: Lost Adirondack Empire,* published in 1988, refutes this epic telling.

This John Brown grew up in Providence, and was on his way to becoming a successful businessman, much to the regret of his father and previous generations of Providence Browns, who had all served as Puritan ministers. But John was determined to make his way in this world first, and was well on his way when troubles with the Mother Country began. And like the later John Brown of the Civil War—no family tie, by the way—our

Revolutionary War John had an intense and passionate soul.

He joined the rebel cause and committed illegal acts, including, of all things, a sympathetic duplication of the Boston Tea Party, during which festivities Brown and some other Patriots—or Hotheads, depending upon your point of view— dumped tea into Providence Harbor. Brown went underground, to emerge fully and safely only after independence had been achieved and acknowledged by the Crown.

Brown returned to his calling, commerce, and became a financial and cultural force in Rhode Island. He helped create and endowed Brown University; he underwrote and created the first State Bank of Rhode Island; his clipper ships were among the first to sail to the East and open up the China trade. Unhappily, his ships, as were others', were converted—after his death—into the infamous Slavers, which violated federal law as well as the English blockade, and ran the horrible Triangle, the passage from Africa to the Indies to the United States.

Brown himself did not live to see this infamy; indeed, his Puritan background might have worked other things, who knows? What we can say is that as a trader in the China market, as a banker, and as a land developer, John Brown became one of the most important members of Rhode Island society.

There were two daughters in the family, one of whom married Frederick Herreshoff, whose fate we've already seen. The other daughter chose a rather weak character as a mate, a lawyer from Philadelphia. He was sheltered within the capable hands of father-in-law Brown's commercial interests. And this is the point at which our story unfolds.

About 1793 or 1794, Brown sent his son-in-law to New York City to oversee the transfer of bills of lading from one of the firm's clipper ships, recently returned to harbor after a three-year journey to the East. The issue was the transfer of the stated value of the cargo—some $200,000—into a bank draft to be delivered to Brown's Rhode Island bank.

In the course of his New York adventure, this "Philadelphia Lawyer" became involved with a cabal of New York land speculators who included among them Philip Livingston, a family name we've run across before, and Aaron Burr, a name known to all of us. The inevitable happened. Almost archetypically, "YOUNG INNOCENT COMES TO BIG CITY AND

GETS FLEECED." The bank draft for $200,000 (more or less) is exchanged for a wonderful tract of newly opened land in the real estate hot spot of the decade: The Great North Woods.

John Brown receives not a bank draft for $200,000; he receives a deed for some 210,000 acres (more or less) of prime real estate. And to add salt to the wounds, it takes years of expensive litigation before Brown can claim a property free of liens and legal complications, from what it is apparent was part of the original Macomb Purchase.

Well, there you are with an awfully expensive bit of wild forest. What do you do? Obviously, try to develop it as much as possible and recoup some of your losses. So around 1799 or 1800, John Brown (who, by the way, had waxed almost as large as his fortune; he weighed, it is reported, close to 300 pounds) set out from the comfort of his home and civilized society and, leaving Providence, made his way to Fort Schuyler, now Utica. Hiring guides, he started up the lakes and streams now joined in name as "The Fulton Chain" (the lakes themselves are now numbered, First through Eighth). He went as far as the waterway named for him, "Brown's Inlet."

John Brown did what every developer will do: map the property, divide it into sections, and name the sections so they can be identified for development and sale. He instructed surveyors to lay out the tract and divide it into eight townships. And coming from a long line of Puritan clergy, Brown had each township named after a Puritan virtue. On older maps and documents we can see these eight townships listed: "INDUSTRY," "ENTERPRISE," "PERSEVERANCE," "UNANIMITY," "FRUGALITY," "SOBRIETY," "ECONOMY," and lastly, a strong contender as my favorite, "REGULARITY."

I am tempted to declare that we can make quite a "to-do" about the fact that these Puritan virtues tend to deal with economic rather than ethical behavior. But perhaps the two were united in Puritan thought. Whatever, I do believe that these names bespeak a type of personality and character that was profoundly involved in the early days of our nation.

And if John Brown was a uniquely successful merchant and landowner of Puritan bent, many Bible-owning settlers were not. If the sight of this Promised Land inspired "Mt. Pisgah," the settling of it has given us "Balm of Gilead Mountain,"

"Jericho," "Galilee," "Moriah" (Moriah is, of course, the mount upon which Abraham showed his total obedience to God by preparing to sacrifice his son, Isaac), "Jordan River," and "Sabbath Day Point" as well as "Sodom." And we could get there on "Kingdom Road" or "Lost Nation Road" or "Jerusalem Road."

There are other names that would have been considered eccentric then, as they are now, and these too tell us about the cast of mind of the people who coined them. In the 1840s there were twin settlements on the east and west sides of Long Lake, the long lake between Tupper and Blue Mountain Lakes. It seems that itinerant peddlers traversing the wild outposts of civilization in the Adirondacks would on occasion show up with trade goods, like sewing needles, cloth products, even some luxuries like bonnets—things they could pack in through the mountains on their backs.

As you might expect, the prices for these goods did not reflect what one might pay when shopping at a downtown emporium. In fact, according to the disgruntled men of the communities, the prices were so exorbitant that they insisted upon calling their settlements "Kickerville" and "Gougeville."

Of course, respectable society would not allow that today, but in the early days of settlement this sort of eccentricity found a place and offers us a glimpse at the quality of mind and emotion among the early settlers.

Well, we've looked at some names and listened to some stories. All aimed at showing how names can tell us as much about the people as about the land. Certainly Biblical names like "Mt. Pisgah" tell us about the namers. And just as surely do Personal names like "Malone" and "Elizabethtown." Names like "Mt. Marcy" give us clues about the prominent people and priorities of the age, and we can read our history in other Commemorative names such as "Washington County." Transfer names like "Madrid" and "Essex" open a window into the emotions of those bringing the name with them. And, of course, the humor of Eccentric names invites us to admire those characters coining them.

Biblical, Personal, Commemorative, Transfer, and Eccentric: these types of names peel back for a moment the curtains of time and allow us a vision of the flesh and blood, the feelings and beliefs of our forefathers.

We've noted the commemorative "Lake Flower," in the village of Saranac Lake. In addition to a fascinating history, which includes serving as an international center for the treatment of tuberculosis, and such inviting annual rituals as the raising and then storming of a towering ice palace during February's Winter Carnival, Saranac Lake has been blessed with a rich sequence of eccentric and personal names. We can learn much about its citizens by seeing what they were willing to call themselves.

The following article was first published in the *Adirondack Daily Enterprise* on August 13, 1986. Mr. John Duquette, the author, is a respected local historian whose writing is so pleasurable that I will quote verbatim from his article. Mr. Duquette and the publisher, Mr. William Doolittle, have kindly allowed me to excerpt the article for our "instruction and delight."

ADIRONDACK DAILY ENTERPRISE
August 13, 1986
"The Saranac Lake House"
by John J. Duquette

Where Lake Street presently meets the shore of Lower Saranac Lake there once existed a fabulous hotel renowned for both its owner and its famous guests. It also played an important role in the history of our village.

During the latter half of the 1800s the desk registers listed such prominent names as Teddy Roosevelt, Vice President, William Almon Wheeler and Governor Levi Morton. From the business world came Macy, Rockefeller, Tiffany, Winchester, Morgenthau and McAlpin among many others. Authors and artists were represented by Henry Van Dyke, Street, Headley and "Adirondack Murray" together with W. J. Stillman and A. F. Tait. Names closely associated with the area: Paul Smith, Dr. E. L. Trudeau, S. R. Stoddard, Verplanck Colvin, W. W. Durant and Thomas Blagden appear with regularity through the pages. Many guests signed in with such renowned guides as Mitchell Sabattis, Alvah Dunning, Mart Moody, Steve Martin, Jesse Corey and John Plumley. Other guides arrived in their guide boats to pick up the patrons arriving by stage coach from AuSable Forks and Elizabethtown. . . .

The name Saranac had been applied to the three lakes, and also to the river which connected them, but had not as yet been applied to the village. The derivation of the world has baffled historians and Indian translators for ages.

Did the name descend downstream from the lakes to the river or was it vice versa? At first it was believed to be an Indian name but William Beauchamp, in his authoritative "Aboriginal Place Names of New York," states that no meaning has been definitely assigned this name. In his history, A. L. Donaldson cites a possible solution to the mystery. The name St. Aranack is shown on an early map to designate a river and from the French pronunciation might have slurred it into Saranac. I'm inclined to agree with Donaldson.

The infant settlement on the river had been called "Harrietstown" and at an earlier date was known simply as "The River." Later movements attempted to name the village in honor of some of its prominent citizens. Among the nominees were "Baker's" for Col. Milote Baker, "Trudeau" for Dr. E. L. Trudeau and "Bloodville" for Orlando Blood. Col. Baker owned a hotel next to the present Pine Street bridge and in 1854 he became the hamlet's first postmaster. The colonel was a firebrand Democrat and when Buchanan lost to Lincoln in 1861, he not only lost his post office to Martin but also lost the opportunity to have his name immortalized in village history.

To this I would merely add these other variations found on early maps: "Serindac," "Salasanac," "Savaniac" and "St. Armand" (perhaps a corruption of St. Martin). Native American contenders include "S'nhalo'nek" and "Salonak." And the land taken by Captain Pliny Miller was sometimes called "Up The River" as well as "The River" to distinguish it from the holdings of the other original settler, Jacob Smith Moody, who took the area called "The Pines" or "Moody's."

So did Saranac Lake evolve: from any one of seven Native American or French names to "Harrietstown" to "The River" or "Up The River" to "Martin's" to "Baker's" to "Trudeau" to "Bloodville" to, finally, "Saranac Lake," incorporated in 1892.

5

Digging With Names

When archaeologists sift through the mud of some river embankment and discover a shard of pottery or a splintered rock worked into some tool or a bit of bone, the degree of excitement often becomes intense. For there is the possibility of hints at the historical experiences of the people who left these traces of themselves. So it is with names: they are the artifacts, the linguistically manufactured goods which often hint at aspects of those who coined them. Often names represented the only or the first clue of a previous civilization. But that was true most often in Europe and other parts of the world where most history is pre-history. That is, where most events were not recorded.

In the Adirondacks, as in most of our country, the languages and, therefore, names (with the exception of Native American) come to us relatively recently, within the last 450 years. That means that names generally are not the only or the first clue to previous times and historical events. Nevertheless, even if names aren't the only key to discovering the past, they often spark the tracing back to some little known—and at times, wished to be forgotten—historical episodes or eras.

We've done some digging with the stories of "Adirondack," "Old Forge," "Raquette," "Macomb's Purchase," "Elizabeth-town," "Fulton Chain," "Brown's Tract," and "Saranac Lake;" let's do some more.

A number of years ago a prominent citizen of Lake Placid learned of my interest in names, and since I had lived in the area through enough winters to qualify as "part native" (one very powerful class distinction in the Adirondacks, which often dominates all other distinctions, is longevity: not mere age, but rather the length of time of permanent habitation in the community), he decided that I was to be "part trusted" with communal information.

Thus I learned that there had been a section of Lake Placid with the name "Timbuktu." Never, of course, on any map or official document: merely an informal, a local designation. If you're ever in Lake Placid, head down to where the Chub River spills over the wooden dam, just beyond the little park on River Street. You'll be in "Timbuktu."

And then, as if to really put me in my place, this respected elder statesman of the village, this paradigm of all that is virtuous in the innocence of small town living said, "And I bet you don't know where Little Chicago is either."

"Little Chicago!" "Timbuktu!" Although the hints seem pretty broad now, I've never been especially good with these kinds of puzzles. It took me a little while to figure out that the John Brown of anti-slavery fame, and Al Capone—of Elliot Ness/FBI fame—were connected to these local names in Lake Placid. And, as my enigmatic but genial friend guessed, these names started me digging. Here's what I came up with. Right from the beginning.

Back in 1792, you'll recall, William Constable managed to sell part of the Macomb Purchase, Great Tract No. 5, to a syndicate of French aristocrats frightened by what seemed to be the imminent fall of the "Old Order." They sent agents to this "Great Tract," to survey it and develop plans for settlements. One of the men, by the way, was Mark Brunel, later connected with the Suez Canal.

Messieurs Brunel, Desjardines and Pharoax made their way north from New York City to Albany and westward along the Mohawk River. At one point they stayed in Fort Schuyler at a tavern operated by a Mr. Peter Smith. The party moved on, and out of our present tale.

Our story picks up with Peter Smith. Some time shortly after the stay of the three French agents for La Compagnie de New York, another guest at the tavern persuaded Smith to give up the hotel/tourist trade and join in an enterprise in the newly opened North Woods to resume the trade for beaver pelts.

Peter Smith allows himself to be persuaded, and after a number of successful years amasses a fortune and sells out his interests to his partner—one John Jacob Astor! Although Smith never achieved the international or social reputation gained by the Astor family and their Hudson's Bay Company, the former innkeeper was able to bestow an enormous legacy upon his son, Gerrit.

Gerrit Smith grew up in that passionate era when religious intensity was at the service of those who hated the fact of American slavery. Gerrit became one of the important financiers of the Abolitionist movement, devoting large sums of his legacy to activities aimed at freeing and developing Black independence. One such project involved creating sanctuaries in which runaway slaves could be hidden safely until transportation to Canada could be arranged (part of the underground railroad system). At the same time these sanctuaries could serve as permanent homes for free Blacks who wished to preserve their independence by farming the land.

Smith used his legacy to purchase large tracts of newly available lands in northern and central New York State. And in 1849 he deeded to John Brown 350 acres of land on the western slope of the "Valley of the AuSable" at North Elba, that which is known as "The Plains of Abraham."

Brown brought his wife, Mary, and his sons and daughters to the farm. He invested his considerable skills as a farmer and husbandryman in the Plains of Abraham, for we must not forget that he had come from a long line of successful Connecticut farming people and had himself shown prize cattle in fairs across New England and in Britain.

But John Brown brought with him more than farming skills. He brought to North Elba that passionate hatred of slavery and that singular love for the slave that we've read about so much in all accounts of this man who is both blessed and reviled for "causing the Civil War." And the pact between him and Gerrit Smith was that his farm would become the training ground for Blacks interested in learning to become self-sufficient farmers here in the North Country. To that purpose John Brown came to North Elba, to a farm literally overlooking Lake Placid.

They farmed the land and lived in cabins which huddled together at the edge of the Chub River. And earlier settlers than these Black families called the cluster of homes "Timbuktu." Years later at a celebration at the grave of John Brown on his farm, now a most attractive museum and visiting spot, a number of the descendants of the inhabitants of "Timbuktu" helped make up those honoring the memory of this martyr to the cause of human freedom and dignity.

Some thirty years after that celebration at John Brown's grave, another period in American life gave rise to another neighborhood in Lake Placid. It seems that the Prohibition Era in America helped create a number of illegal enterprises in the Adirondacks. Not much bathtub gin was actually made up here, but many of our citizens devoted themselves to ensuring that the major East Coast cities, including New York's capital as well as the Big Apple, did not suffer from a scarcity of the excellent Canadian whiskey just north of the border.

Since the hint was first dangled before me, I have sounded out a number of longtime inhabitants of Lake Placid and Saranac Lake about the whereabouts of this "Little Chicago." Surely the notoriety of the Chicago kingpin of organized crime, Al Capone, had led our industrious locals to call the section of town where the booze was stored "Little Chicago." Generally the responses I get when nosing around are mischievous expressions as Placidians boast of a father or uncle or grandfather and the highjinks of eluding the authorities while moving the whiskey along the pipeline to the nation's speakeasies. I still don't know where "Little Chicago" was.

"Timbuktu" and "Little Chicago" have little in common other than as they illustrate how a name can get you digging into the past and the mysteries that can be brought to light.

I often wonder what people will think a hundred years from now when they ask in 2089 how Lake Placid got its name. We can tell them, with the help of a little digging, that a somewhat idyllically inclined tourist suggested that "Bennet's Pond" was much too prosaic a name for that which offered such a soulful balm to the spirit. And, we can add, the thought that some future visitors might feel that "Lake Placid" is much too much a beehive of activity to be considered "placid," would have been inconceivable to our early name-giver. One can visualize a scene in the future when people actually question the integrity of our citizens in using a term like "placid" to describe this "Olympic Village."

It is the growing disparity between the name and its meaning—its opaqueness, you'll recall—that started me digging back to Mr. Bennet and his pond.

Another disparity, this time in terms of languages, spurred me on to another site and another "dig." When I was trying to work out the Scottish ending to Mr. Platt's settlement, I was struck by the curious flow of two French river names into Lake Champlain, one a bit north and the other directly south of the English/Scottish town of Plattsburgh. "Ausable" is relatively easy. It's translucent enough in English—"to the sand," obviously referring to the sandy shores of its mouth as it empties into Lake Champlain. But why "Chazy?" We'll have to dig for that one.

Let's dig deep into the past, as far back as the 1640s during the time of discovery, conflict, the pressing of French and English claims and the posturing for ownership of this part of the new world. The time of Iroquoian and Algonkian presence in the Adirondacks.

At a time we usually describe as a lull in the periodic outbreak of attacks between the English and their Iroquoian allies on the one hand, and the French and their Algonkian allies on the other, it seems, we are told, that the aristocratic nephew of the governor of Montreal went south into the Adirondacks on a hunting expedition with a band of Algonkians. They were set upon by a party of Mohawks with the unhappy result the death of the young French nobleman, his long blond hair the trophy of the war chief.

The governor was distraught, of course, but there was nothing he could do other than mourn the loss of his nephew. This was the price of opening up a new world, even during a period of "peace."

A year later there was arranged a major conference, a "pow wow," in Montreal, which by the way is a contracted form of "Mont Royal." The goal of the meeting was a peace agreement so that the fur trade could be carried on. The French needed good relations with the Iroquois. This name, "Iroquois," by the way, is the French word for the Five Nation Confederacy (Mohawk, Oneida, Onondaga, Cayuga and Seneca).

Unfortunately, war chiefs as well as political leaders came to the meeting (the two roles were never joined in the same person). Over a period of days, gifts were exchanged, dinners were held, speeches were made, and understandings were arrived at. But while all this was going on a Mohawk war chief was proudly displaying his collection of hair pieces taken in battle.

Of course, the governor's people reported the ominous likeness of one of these gruesome mementos to the fair head of the lost nephew. Despite grim and suspicious looks and hints from the French, the war chief continued to enjoy his stay, and at a particularly jovial celebration he boasted that he had taken the fair-haired scalp at a river which soon ran into the "great inland sea," that is, Lake Champlain. He went on to describe the foolish young "white eyes."

The governor maintained his composure throughout the grizzly tale, concluded the conference with vows of eternal friendship, watched the Mohawk leave Montreal for their home near Albany . . . and planned his revenge.

Through the days of the following winter the governor set about equipping and organizing a strike force composed of his French countrymen and Algonkian allies. They marched in late winter, before the snows melt and the ice thaws. South over Lake Champlain and down Lake George they marched, and taking the Mohawk settlement by surprise, they took their revenge. The entire settlement was destroyed. Thus ended the peace treaty and trade agreement; thus eased the governor's rage, if not his sorrow, and thus ends this little tale.

If the story smacks of the folktale, with its tragic killing, suppressed need for vengeance, drunken Indian who gives himself away, and a climax of a frightful bloodletting, you are quite right. Almost all folk legend involving White and Native American violence seems to revolve around revenge taken for a violent crime against a White. And the revenge is brought about by the drunken bravado of the Native American. But then, these are White folktales, not Iroquois.

It is almost unnecessary to say, but on the off chance that the story was so beguiling that the point has been obscured, the site of the murder of the young French nobleman with the flowing golden hair was a river bank whose waters empty into Lake Champlain somewhat north of Plattsburgh. And the nobleman's name? Chazy, of course.

That the period of English and French contention in the Adirondacks was horribly vicious and brutal is well known; but less than well understood is its duration. The war(s) between the White and Native American partners (French and Algonkian opposed to English and Iroquoian) continued on and off for over one hundred years, culminating only in the last five years of the 1750–1760 decade. It was during these years that such names as "Lake George" emerged, as we have seen, from "La Lac du Sacrement."

In this same period and in the same neighborhood (more or less), there rests a lovely and peaceful, a most idyllic pool of water, with the unhappy name of "Bloody Pond." As you can imagine, only a little digging was necessary to uncover the remains of the carnage that took place here during one of the battles between the French and English and their allies. The bodies of the wounded and dead, in the waters of this peaceful pond, gave name to the water. Not "bloody," as in the English slang, "You bloody fool," but rather as a description, however gruesome, of the crimson waters running with the blood from the wounds of the dead and dying.

There is another small body of water with the unhappy name "Calamity Pond." And although the events which led to this name were not as nationally significant as those that were part of the struggle between French and English interests in the Adirondacks, they were, indeed, profoundly crucial to the history of a family and an entire Adirondack industry. In a way, the monument erected in the wilderness near "Calamity Pond" by the family of David Henderson is a tribute to the iron age in the Adirondacks as well as to one of its founding families. And when one digs about to uncover the facts behind "Calamity Pond," the stories that emerge touch upon iron ore and pioneers and Native Americans and Adirondack guides.

Our story really begins way back in 1826 on the edge of the Chub River in Lake Placid, not far at all from where the cabins were put up giving rise to "Timbuktu." But long before "Timbuktu" men had discovered rich veins of iron ore, and foundries had sprung up throughout the Adirondacks: remember the "Old Forge" in the "Brown's Tract." Stretches along the Saranac River were dotted with foundries and kilns. In Essex County, there were clusters of mines along Lake Champlain, and don't forget Gilliland's foundry used for the American fleet in Lake Champlain. And by 1808 iron was being mined deep in the Adirondacks along the Chub River. The life of the Adirondacks in the last century was inseparably linked to the mining and processing of iron ore. Iron and timber were to that century what recreation and vacations are to this one.

By 1826, Archibald McIntyre and his son-in-law, David Henderson, were faced with the decreased productivity of their operation on the Chub River. The ore was less available and the cost of transporting charcoal from the kilns reduced profits too much. The legend is that they were approached one day as they were about to shut the works down. A Native American by the name of Sabael (some contend it was his son, Lewis Elijah) showed them a sample of ore—really a rock of ore—so heavy with iron that both men were astonished. It seems the Native American, always curious about the minerals he ran across in his wanderings, had stumbled across some of this very heavy "rock" while crossing a stream. He recognized it as something that would be of interest to the men at the iron mine at the Chub River.

McIntyre and Henderson and a few others followed Sabael or Elijah through what is known as "Indian Pass" to a natural dam of almost pure iron ore in an area later to be known as the "Upper Works" and "Lower Works." Whether or not the party kept their guide Sabael/Elijah under wraps while they staked their claim in Albany is fanciful conjecture. What we do know is that this discovery led to the most active mining operation in the High Peaks, The Adirondack Iron Works.

The "Upper Works" and the "Lower Works" generated so much activity that a number of Irish immigrants came into the area to join the local "Yankee" population in the mining, transporting, and processing of the ore. A village emerged and the typical "company town" developed, in which a paternalistic benevolence reinforced just those social distinctions our democratic inclinations want to erase. ("The Company Town" in the democratic Adirondacks would make a fine book. But back to our story.) When the mine did finally close, the "Ironworks" became known as "The Deserted Village."

Ultimately the costs of transportation, of moving the ore and iron some thirty miles to Lake Champlain, and other factors led to the gradual closing of the operation. But before that unhappy time, David Henderson was instrumental in seeing that the mines stayed open and that the village thrived. By all accounts, Henderson was a vigorous and forceful man.

And he enjoyed the pleasures of the hunt and the company of one of the most famous of early Adirondack guides, John Cheney. The legend tells of a day's outing during which—and here the tale gets a bit fuzzy, as is understandable—either a cocked pistol went off as it was being passed from Henderson to Cheney, or Henderson dropped his jacket to the ground, for the day was quite warm, and his pistol fired. Whatever the version, the outcome was the same: David Henderson died from an accidental pistol shot while on an outing with his guide. This calamity occurred in September of 1845.

Years later the family erected a monument to Henderson's memory at the spot in the wilderness where the accident occurred, near the shores of "Calamity Pond." The pond bears witness to this most distressing family and personal tragedy. At the same time, Henderson's accidental death hastened the final end of the "Ironworks."

Iron mines, Adirondack guides, the "Indians," McIntyre and Henderson: all uncovered while we dig around "Calamity Pond."

One more story, out of so many at hand, will show us how names can help us uncover the past. There is a township and village, "Santa Clara," deep in the heart of Adirondack lumbering country, not too far from that hub of French Canadian lumbering and railroading activity, Tupper Lake. By the way, the insightful historian of Tupper Lake, Louis Simon, in his tribute to the forces which made the village so prominent, titled his book, *Mostly Spruce and Hemlock.* This reference to the local answer to inquiries about the village's population illustrates the joys of keeping one's ear tuned to local wisdom and the ways of expressing it.

I once interviewed an elderly gentleman, a former lumberman. He told me that when he came to Tupper Lake in 1912 from Three Rivers in Quebec, "if you didn't speak French, you'd starve." But even before the turn of the century, as far back as the 1870s when the Adirondacks supplied the East Coast with the timber needed to build the expanding industrial and urban complexes after the Civil War, even as far back as that, Tupper Lake was a hub of timbering activity.

And outside Tupper Lake, in the woods, a Mr. John Hurd was carving out a series of lumbering camps and employing a great number of French Canadian lumbermen to cut and trim and peel and move the logs to the saw mills. His extensive land holdings were in what he chose to name "Santa Clara," a wonderfully Spanish and exotically romantic name for an Adirondack forest.

A new level of technology had finally come to this remote section of the Adirondacks: railroads. This was crucial to the timbering way of life. For one thing, before rails came into the woods only softwoods like spruce and pine could be cut for the markets because only softwoods would float in the river drives. The oaks and beeches would sink. With railroads, the rich stands of hardwoods could be cut and moved to the mills.

So John Hurd, owner of large tracts of forest lands, began building a main line with branches. He ultimately linked about sixty miles (more or less) of railroad line, stringing together all his camps and connecting them to the mills and terminus in Tupper Lake.

Hurd was, from all reports, quite a character. A religious man, it is said he used to go from camp to camp on a Sunday morning, rousing his lumbermen to go to church services and running a "church" train. Yet, as a successful "boss," it is said that his "company stores" were so efficient that sometimes his lumberjacks ended the season in debt to the store after paying off their "chits" from their accumulated salaries. His foremen, it is charged, were adroit at discouraging the Lebanese peddlers who trekked up from Utica in the hopes of trading in the lumbering camps.

It is also said that Hurd at one time agreed to sell his sixty miles of line to William Seward Webb, son-in-law to Cornelius Vanderbilt. Webb was in the process of building a railway line from Utica to Montreal and considered using Hurd's already operating sixty miles of rail rather than laying another line in such a wastefully parallel track. The agreed-upon price was $600,000, an impressive figure in an age of no income taxes and a dollar worth mountains of what it is worth today.

The story goes on that Hurd backed out of the deal at the

last moment and tried to hold Webb up for a cool million. Webb is reputed to have objected angrily to being "blackmailed" and having a verbal understanding suddenly broken. He vowed to "break" Hurd. Vanderbilt's son-in-law then went on to build a line parallel to Hurd's, and with its access to Utica and Canada—hence all the markets and urban centers, including Albany and New York City via the connection with the New York Central Railroad—Webb took away all of Hurd's business, other than the timber. Since even that became less available as the cutting went on without plans for reforestation, Hurd's empire ultimately collapsed, and Webb was able, indeed, to see Hurd go out of business.

But that failure did not change the name of the township in which so much of Hurd's empire was based. He had called the place "Santa Clara," and it remains so today. When the waters that flow through such places in "Santa Clara" as "St. Regis Falls" are stilled by the cold of winter, one can think of the Trade Winds and salt water breezes and soft warm waves of the tropic waters of Santa Clara's original. But Hurd was not thinking so much of winter's escape via "Club Med" or some other travel agency. He was thinking of the woman he loved and had married. He was thinking of his wife's birthplace and his desire to honor her. Thus, "Santa Clara."

6

That's A Folktale!

[ET · Y · MOL · O · GY] (rhymes with "wet apology"): "The history of a linguistic form . . ." says *Webster's Ninth,* and it is sufficient for us as a start. Yes, the history of the form of a word, or of course of a name. Its spelling, pronunciation, meaning, origin. In fact what we've been doing all along is flirt with etymology.

But this kind of label is often less useful than it might be, and to talk about what we've been doing in terms of ETYMOLOGY would have, I think, made us somewhat skittish, like an adolescent on a first date. No, better for us to have approached the subject flying confidently under the banner of COMMON SENSE than to have played the overly awed suitor happy for a glimpse of his beloved ETYMOLOGY.

And so for five chapters now we've been looking at names on the Adirondack landscape, seeing in them glimpses of the people and the episodes which have made this land as remarkable as its mountains and waters. But here we must give pause and face up to etymology, for understanding that She offers us a description of the history of words and names will allow us to understand her cousin, FOLK ETYMOLOGY.

You see, one aspect of folk culture, as opposed to, for example, reading this book, is that information is passed ("transmitted," to borrow a term from high-tech culture) by word of mouth, what is called the "oral tradition." This notion of passing the information and wisdom of a culture from one generation to the next by hearing it told to you and remembering it so that you can tell it to your children is at the heart of any notion of folk culture.

Now, many names, as you can imagine, were coined and became part of the Adirondack landscape before things were written down in a language we could understand. Native American names come to mind, of course. But many names of French and English origin were also coined and became part of our landscape, part of our "name vocabulary" before they were recorded in official documents, especially in places with sparse populations, places that had not attracted development and settlement. Thus it has happened that information about a name, the who, when and why, was known only by those who cared to remember the stories about those places.

When students of names (we call ourselves ONOMAST-ICIANS from the Greek *Onoma,* Name, and by the way, ONOMASTICIANS love ETYMOLOGIES) began going beyond the written documents or beyond the components of the name itself (our "Essex" for example, or "ville") and began investigating names whose documents and forms lacked sufficient information or clues, we took to the field. We onomasticians took to the field (as all good students do) and began by talking to people who lived in or near those places. In fact, when language scientists left the laboratory and went out into the field, they found that talking to people in the communities was most worthwhile when patterned on the techniques of talking to people (in the jargon, called "informants") devised by generations of anthropologists, regional dialect collectors and folklorists. And this leads us to the label "Folk Etymology."

Consider this scene: a student of place names approaches an individual. Now the conventional wisdom—which in this case makes just good common sense—is that you talk to older people in the community. After all, they've lived through longer times and will remember more of those times. You can test this theory easily: just ask college students anything about anything that happened before 1970. They'll almost universally answer with a shake of the head; after all, they weren't born until after that.

So you find those people in the community who have lived through a good many years and through different times and who have acquired reputations for "knowing a lot about the old days." Now, this reputation enhances the status of the informants; it indicates that they have something special to offer—and they do! It works both ways. Informants are one of the most valuable resources we have for learning about the past. At the same time, when we approach informants, we give them one more opportunity to contribute to their community, to give of themselves.

It is a wonderful and satisfying give and take. But we must be very careful. Continue to consider the scene. You've identified your informant, reinforcing his or her importance. Now you ask about a name. You know, "how did it get that name?" "who called it that first?" "what does that name mean?" And you wait for the answer, pen and notebook at the ready.

Your informant, we know, has a great many valuable memories to share and a great deal of important information to pass on to you, the next generation; but of all the things to ask about, your informant really doesn't know about that one blasted name you brought up!

But your informant wants to please you, wants to see your excitement as you acquire all this "lost" information. Your informant wants to maintain the reputation that brought you to him or her, wants to ensure that you'll return for some more information. Your informant might even want to have some fun with you, say something to tell the others to show what a card he or she is.

So it may be that the question about a name is answered with a little stretching of the prosaic into the dramatic, or the making up of what seems plausible from the sound of the name itself. Or the telling of an old story about the place or about the name just to entertain you or pull your leg. *Anything* except the admission of not knowing. Thus we come to an etymology based upon spoken, i.e., oral information. And that, when it smacks of the folk imagination, is what we have come to call folk etymology.

You know, when we look back at some of the names we've talked about, folk etymology comes to mind. "Kickerville" and "Gougeville" are suspiciously "folksy" in their etymologies, aren't they? But let's look at a place still known in Tupper Lake, a very small point of land in the water, called "Sally's Rock."

Sometimes true love creates place-names. It seems that around 1848 Sally Cole, daughter of one of Tupper Lake's first settlers, came to that age when she should be married. And she set her cap on a fellow named "Aire." Now Aire really didn't have much of a chance once Sally determined on him, and before long they were planning the wedding. However, there wasn't a proper minister in the entire area, and so Sally had to exhibit a good deal of patience. Aire seemed less upset about it.

One day a timber cruiser came into town. (That's the fellow who goes before the logging crew and marks the trees to be cut.) And he happened to be a preacher as well. When Sally found that out, plans for the wedding rushed to completion. The day was set, the food was cooked, everyone was invited, and Mr. Cole ordered the barrel of good rye whiskey made available.

The day arrived and things moved along as planned. The pre-nuptial eating and drinking and dancing and general merrymaking were going along swimmingly. Then somebody told Aire that the preacher man had come across Tupper's Lake from St. Lawrence County and couldn't marry anyone outside of it. Aire took a big swallow from Mr. Cole's whiskey dipper and broke the sad news to Sally.

Well, this determined young lady organized a flotilla. All the guests followed Sally and Aire and the preacher man and Sally's father and the whiskey barrel. And they rowed up Tupper's Lake till they came to the first island they reckoned was in St. Lawrence County. And on that island Sally and Aire were married. That's how come folks call that place "Sally's Rock."

Some names and folktales are married as profoundly as are Sally and Aire!

There is another island in Big Tupper Lake whose features have conjured up not the happy images of love, but the terror and hate of Satan. According to Native American legend, and interestingly enough, a legend emerging only after the introduction of the White man's religion in the Adirondacks, the Devil appears once a year in the deepest part of the frozen winter. He stands upon the edge of a sheer, rocky bluff on the island and preaches to those assembled shivering on the frozen lake below. The island is known as "Devil's Pulpit."

It is oral legend that gives us "Sally's Rock" and "Devil's

Pulpit." The vast reservoir of human sensibility and creativity called "folklore" is the rich soil in which these name explanations . . . oops, I mean etymologies, grow. Names are always created by and connected to people, and the legends that produce names and their explanations are found throughout the Adirondacks.

There is "Rogers' Rock," on the northern end of Lake George, from which Captain Rogers, of French and Indian War fame, escaped a band of "redskins" (not redcoats) hot on his heels and dripping with war paint by leaping from his rock into Lake George. Of course the "redskins," being mere mortals, could not presume to equal this superhumanly Olympian feat. They stopped, disgruntled, and Captain Rogers (I almost forget myself and said "Captain Marvel") went on to other exploits.

The facetiousness of my tone is not meant to deny the vitality of these sorts of exploits, even in fiction. For these stories, this "folklore" cracks open a bit the doors to our past. These stories help us understand how we saw the world and how we felt about the world and how we dreamed the world might be. Rogers Rangers gave us many things. One of them is "Rogers' Rock."

Other names lend themselves to wonderfully wry comments, evoking the "North Country" humor. Approximately two miles from Vermontville, east towards Plattsburgh on Route 3, lies a horseshoe side road called by the locals "Sink Hole Road," a name finally made official by state road signs. My informant's words are worth our attention.

> Sink Hole, that's just what it is. One story about it is some fool apparently tried to take a short cut across his property. He was driving a wagon and a two-horse hitch when he started down the hill next to the brook or swampy place there. When he tried to cross the small brook, the wagon mired down and sank from sight in the mud. The state highway went through the Sink Hole and every year since then, the pavement sinks two, three inches.

Other residents add that there is as much as four feet of pavement resting in the Sink Hole today!

Another road conjures up the days of the "Grand Hotels" in the Adirondacks. There is a road running between Paul Smiths and Gabriels which intersects Bert LaFountain Road. Now Bert, by the way, is a local legend. Actually, he was a legend in his own time, and not many legends can say that for themselves. Bert was the great Prohibition hero of the region. As close to a Robin Hood as we've ever had.

We've got a song about Bert and his escapades (we like to think of them as "high jinks"), called *Bert LaFountain's Packard.* This folksong runs on and on for almost as many verses outwitting the Border Patrol and the revenuers as there were miles put on Bert's Packard doing it! And we've got wonderful stories of Bert giving the local parish priest handsome Sunday contributions with the wry note that he felt a bit guilty because more parishioners were at his "speakeasy" than at Mass.

But before we turned on to Bert LaFountain Road, we were driving along from Paul Smiths to Gabriels. That road is "Easy Street." Intrigued by that name, I drove out there a number of years ago. Then, the size of the pot holes I was told were always present made it less of an easy street. Now the road is very smooth and makes its name understandable. But that's not how it came to be called "Easy Street."

There was a time in the 1880s when this road fronted the cottages of many of the guides who worked for Paul Smith and served the guests at his hotel. These chosen few, these Adirondack guides, did work very hard, but their wages were immense: three dollars a day. Now, there were days when guests at Paul Smiths could look out over the balconies of the hotel and see these rough-hewn men, at times lounging about, seeming to own the world. On top of that, these wealthy guests were paying top dollar to stay at the hotel and fish and hunt. And they knew (or thought they knew) that after the vacation and they were back at work in their offices, these guides would continue to fish and hunt, *and be paid for doing what they wanted to do,* having made enough money in the summer to be on Easy Street the rest of the year!

Perhaps in momentary envy, perhaps from an imagined simpleness of the life of an Adirondack guide, perhaps from the sense that these men were paid for doing what they liked doing, perhaps a mix of these and other things, but somewhere along the line these wealthy sportsmen decided that their Adirondack guides lived on "easy street."

And now, one more example of folk etymology. This is a

type we'll all recognize: The Bad Pun Type.

Meandering its way through the hills and down toward its entrance into the St. Lawrence River is the waterway called the Oswegatchie River, and the "s" is pronounced as a "z." The local wits will pull your leg with great pleasure when they tell you that the river got its name when a Mohawk was chasing an enemy. After many a narrow escape from the clutches of the Mohawk (not as narrow as Captain Rogers' flight) through the wilds of the mountains and woods, the object of the redskin's wrath tried to ford a river. The Mohawk cut around one of the many bends in the stream and caught his enemy with the triumphant cry, "UGH! I'S A GOTCH YE."

You're right. It's a terrible pun, and the sort of thing that gives folk etymology a bad name!

Now, by all accounts the "Oswegatchie" appears to have come from a Native American word meaning approximately "black river." But most rivers do have dark color on them somewhere. So later on we'll take a look at how Native Americans tended to name their waterways. Certainly not by "I'S A GOTCH YE."

Folklore in the Adirondacks is a rich and, unfortunately, in many ways unknown area. And I'm not sure why. Unless it is that, ironically enough, high-tech Madison Avenue will need to discover it first. When they do, the ad men and fashion designers will have a rich and varied crop to pick from.

There is, of course, our Nat Foster, our first comic book hero disguised as The Deerslayer. There is Old Mountain Phelps of Keene Valley, who in his last years as an octogenarian was still taking (and talking of, as he put it) his "mountaineous walks." There is Honest John Plumley, immortalized by Adirondack Murray, who always went "perpendicular into the woods."

In our own time there is Noah John Rondeau, of Cold River fame. In addition to Noah John's reputation, of a public nature, I've been told of another quality. It seems Noah John and bath water were mortal enemies. "Bathless Groggans" of my youth's Sunday funny paper world was fastidious compared to Noah John Rondeau. I've been told that Noah John smelled so ripe so often that his hermitage was encouraged and applauded by the world out of self-defense rather than philosophic approval. But again, that may be "mere" folktale.

There are all the wonderful stories of enormous fish begging to be hooked and deer inviting the shot. There are the tales of grand living at the palatial summer "camps" of the Rockefellers, Whitneys, Vanderbilts, Posts. There are the stories of Joseph Bonaparte eating dainties on gold-edged dishes in woods still inhabited by wolves, panthers, even moose.

Finally, let's not forget one of the most universal of myths (an up-scale term for folklore) about the Adirondacks: its curative powers. This notion has been described so enthusiastically that the Adirondacks might be called the ultimate elixir. Let's look at one description, from E. Wallace's introduction to his *Guide,* written in 1896.

> The entire Adirondack region is one Vast Sanitarium. The pure and invigorating atmosphere, peculiar to high altitudes, is here highly charged with ozone, and is redolent of the healing aroma of the evergreens; and, among the frequenters of the locality, there are numerous witnesses to its tonic power, which generally affords speedy relief to invalids, and often effects permanent cures. Constitutions enfeebled by anxiety, over-taxation of the brain, and loss of vital energy, sufferers from dyspepsia, chronic nervousness, and some forms of rheumatism, are usually restored to their normal condition, by a sojourn of several weeks or months within its boundaries. The climate is peculiarly beneficial to those suffering with hay-fever, and asthmatic affections, and the fame of the Adirondacks, both as a summer and winter resort for consumptives, is already widespread.

7

Mirror, Mirror, On The Map

> The area is a vast elevated plateau that rises into lofty mountain peaks in the interior, but which slopes gradually down on every side into deep depressions or valleys. . . . The water which runs down and out of the mountains creates boundries which make of the area an island.
>
> Sylvester, pp. 41–45

Whatever the last hundred years have brought in the way of making the wilderness more hospitable, or rather more amenable to creature comforts, such as electricity, power tools, automobiles, snow blowers, inboard motorboats, thermal underwear, ski lifts, central heating, in short, in all the ways we've developed to be able to enjoy the natural beauty of this rugged land, whatever we've done in this regard, a part of us continues to see the Adirondacks as a place of mountains and cascading waters, of isolated lakes and secluded brooks, of hidden trails in forests. In short, and especially for the visitor, the Adirondacks are High Peaks and waterways.

Let's look at these two dominating physical characteristics of the Adirondacks and see what names they were given, what responses to the grand heights and swift, clear water were evoked in our early pioneers and settlers. Let's see how our forefathers saw the landscape of mountains and water.

We must begin, as did the earliest of explorers and settlers, with the waterways. They were then, as they are now, central to the Adirondack experience. Drinking water and care for crops and farm animals were, of course, crucial concerns for our first settlers. But in addition, the lakes and streams served as transportation systems, highways for people and goods. The lumbering industry, for example, depended entirely upon the waterways until the 1870s when railroads came into the mountains. In fact, sections of a great many of our Adirondack rivers such as the Salmon, Saranac, Ausable and Raquette were declared, by numerous legislative acts in Albany, "Public Highways."

Early days saw the settlements in many parts of the Adirondacks determined by the patterns of water flow and current. Mills for grain and timber depended entirely upon waterfalls. Later, the excitement of the promises of electricity depended again on waterfalls. Throughout the history of the Adirondacks visitors enriched the life of the region as they took pleasure in boating, fishing and swimming in the waters of the Adirondacks.

So the major waterways and lakes, the larger rivers and streams, the isolated ponds and brooks became known and enjoyed and used and mapped and, of course, named. And there were some *twenty-seven hundred* (more or less) bodies of water with their own names that we have listed. There are some others named, yet still to be recorded!

Now a goodly number—actually a very large majority, over 80% or more than four out of every five—are personal or descriptive, that is, named for somebody or for some trait of the waterway itself, such as its size or shape, its plant life or animal residents.

We encounter throughout the Adirondacks the likes of "Johns Brook," "Jimmy Creek," "Peters Pond," "Tupper Lake," "Lawrence Brook," "McBride Pond," "Hays Brook," "Follensby Pond," and on and on and on. By and large, these waterways are of modest size and limited commercial or historical importance; so the common man has a chance for immortality, and the brook where he fishes or the pond upon whose bank he builds his cabin allows him to imprint himself into the landscape.

You'll notice, however, that it was a man's world—at least in this regard—and very few women's names were given to these "common" waters. Occasionally a prominent figure such as William Seward Webb would commemorate the love for a woman, calling a wonderful lake "Lila," after his wife. But, don't forget, his wife was the daughter of Cornelius Vanderbilt. For the most part the names of these "lesser" waterways are male and relatively common, despite the odd "Jenny Lake" or "Lydia Pond."

The descriptive water names are generally straightforward, often monosyllabic and unromantic. Good, solid Anglo-Saxon description, as befits the common man. "Beaver Flow," "Big Pond," "Rock Lake," "Wolf Creek," "Upper Duck Hole," "Grass Pond," "Crystal Brook," "Loon Lake," "Hot Water Pond," "Trout Brook," "Polliwog Pond," "Elbow Pond," "Bullhead Pond," and on and on and on. The majority of these water names (hydronym is the fancy term), whether descriptive or personal, are very "down to earth."

But some are different. A few are episodic, in that they remind us of an event and a story, either personal or historic (sometimes both). "Calamity Pond" witnessed the accidental shooting and death of David Henderson, you'll remember. You'll also recall the horror of all the deaths of Mohawk, Algonkian, French, and English/American at "Bloody Pond." There is in Lewis County a reasonably secluded place known as "Sunday Swamp," surely a name to remind us of an episode. And there is on Lake George a "Sabbath Day Point," not connected, I am sure, with the YMCA camp somewhat to the south of it.

Some other water names are reminders of Native American presence in the Adirondacks, if only in the settlers' imagination. You see, conventional wisdom has it that neither the Algonkian nor the nations of the Iroquois Confederacy, particularly the Mohawk, planted permanent settlements in the Adirondacks. Rather, it is believed, Native Americans used the area as a hunting ground and used the waterways as transportation systems. By the way, waterways are just as valuable as transportation systems in the winter as in the seasons when the water is flowing. One cannot use boats, but one can move over the iced surfaces in what become natural corridors unhampered by trees or root systems or rocks.

So it is felt that there were no permanent settlements by Native Americans in the Adirondacks before the white man

came. Let me put you on notice, however, that this crucial
historical and cultural issue is open to debate. Check your maps
and find the name "Onchiota" in Franklin County, most easily
reached for those touring the area off Route 3 between
Plattsburgh and Saranac Lake. Just on the edge of this edenic
community of 79 people (more or less) and two soreheads,
according to the welcoming sign, just on this edge of paradise is
located The Six Nation Indian Museum. Go there! If you want a
sense of the life, the texture of living in and with a tradition that
goes back into the dust of the earliest of days, and the life that
goes on now, then go to this mecca of Mohawk and Iroquois
life.

Founded and perpetuated by the vision and knowledge and
strength of Mr. Ray Fadden, a living legend among many
Mohawks, and his son John Fadden, an artist and now
repository of much of the lore within his father, your tour of the
Adirondacks will be poorer in spirit should you not visit with the
Faddens.

And John insists that were we interested enough in the issue
of the accuracy of Mohawk oral tradition (folklore, to us), we
would trace Mohawk oral records and we would uncover the
evidence of permanent Mohawk settlement. But for now we'll
leave that for the archaeologists.

What we can say on the evidence of the names on the
Adirondack landscape is that the number of place names with
reference to "Indian" is intriguing. I don't mean those names
like "Ticonderoga" and "Saratoga" that are based upon Native
American words. No, I'm referring to "Indian" names.

In addition to the number of names of land characteristics,
such as "Indian Point," "Indian Pass," "Indian Mountain,"
"Mohawk Ridge," and "Mount Iroquois," there are scattered
throughout the Adirondacks the likes of "Indian Brook,"
"Indian Falls," "Indian Lake," and "Indian Creek." In
duplicates! We even have a "Joe Indian Pond" and "Joe Indian
Outlet" as well as a more respectable "Lake Algonquin" or
"Indian River." Let's not overlook the less respectable "Squaw
Brook," "Squaw Lake" and "Squaw Creek."

These names suggest a psychic, if not objective, sense of the
presence of those who lived or traveled through the Adirondacks
before we got here.

Other water names bear witness to the "melting pot" quality of the American/Adirondack experience. In addition to personal names given to waterways whose ethnic background is reflected in the personal name itself, such as the French "Ouleout Creek," the Irish "Donnelly Brook," and the Dutch "Van Derwacker Pond," there are lots of "French Ponds," "Frenchmans Creeks," "Frenchs Brooks." And we are not restricted to the Gauls. "Scotch Lake," "Irish Brook" and "Russian Lake" attest to the strength of the attraction of the new world to peoples of the old one.

There is one more sort of mixing in water names, and this one is alive with possibilities for enriching our language and culture. One name illustrates the mix of the English and French languages in describing a land mass in a lake: "La Rock." Another mixes the English word for another nationality with the Dutch word for "valley" to produce a name of a body of water. So in Hamilton County there is a waterway with the unlikely name of "Frenchs Vly." Talk about opaqueness as well as language mixing! And let's not forget the many English names for streams with the real Dutch suffix "kill" added in such waterways as "Snook Kill," "Owl Kill," "Moses Kill" and the illustrations of opaqueness in names like "Dippkill Pond" and "Copper Kill Pond." The melting pot of water names includes the mixing of languages as well as the mixing of peoples.

Thus far we've seen water names that are personal, that emerge from those common names of common people who came to the Adirondacks to live here. A few water names are episodic, reminding us of personal and familial events or recalling to us major and public moments in the life of the state or nation. There are also Native American water names, a surprising number of them for people who are supposed not to have settled here. And we've looked at the mix of people and languages in our water names, a mix that points to the vital and dynamic ebb and flow of peoples and cultures washing ashore and claiming a part of these Adirondacks.

There is yet one other type of water name, which, however limited in examples, touches upon mighty waters and bears witness to a great many of the crucial historical scenes played out in the Adirondacks. These bodies of water boast names that commemorate those who have affected the life of the region or nation in major ways.

There is the great "Hudson River" itself. Originally the "Groote River" (Great River) or "North River" or "Mauritius" (after the Dutch Prince Maurice) or "Nassau River" (since Prince Maurice came from Nassau), this magnificent waterway became known for the Englishman who first explored its grandeur. The English insisted upon the name "Hudson" for the river, even before they forced the Dutch to accept British control. They too knew the power of the name!

In the same summer when Hudson was moving up the river to explore as far north as the Albany area, the summer of 1609, Samuel de Champlain was heading south from the settlement of what is now Quebec City on the St. Lawrence River. Champlain came as far south as the tip of the "great inland sea" his Algonkian guides had talked about. The legend maintains that as the French and Algonkian party moved farther south, the French became more and more intrigued with the vision of the waterways and mountains (you can, of course, see the High Peaks from the lake), while their Algonkian guides became more and more fearful of discovery by their hereditary enemies, the Mohawk.

Finally, at what is now the Fort Ticonderoga area at the southern tip of the lake, the Mohawk did indeed attack and were in a fair way to do in the Algonkian interlopers. This is when, legend tells us, Champlain and his white comrades opened fire with arquebuses. The Mohawks, never before seeing guns, were at first mystified, and then, as some war chiefs fell with bloody holes in them, terrified. They are reputed to have fled the scene, an act in Mohawk society comparable only to that of a Kamikaze pilot landing his plane and surrendering.

The legend goes on to the effect that this incident led to continued enmity on the part of the Iroquois toward the French for the next one hundred and fifty years. As always, such legends contain just enough truth to allow them to be perpetuated; unfortunately, they contain too much non-truth to be believed fully.

Whatever the felicity of legend, we are safe in noting that 1609 was a watershed year. Hudson edged north along the river that ultimately bore his name, and Champlain fought his way south on the lake that would bear his. Thus, 1609 proclaims the presence of the European world in the Adirondacks, and the river and lake upon which so much of the story of the Adirondacks gets told ultimately became the "Hudson River" and "Lake Champlain."

But even before that crucial year of 1609, a voyage was recorded, you'll recall, that set the stage for all future events in the Adirondacks, Jacques Cartier's 1535 discoveries. Thus it is that the flow from the heartland of America, crashing out over the falls at Niagara, ultimately to spill into the Atlantic Ocean, became known as the St. Lawrence River. It, along with the Hudson River and Lake Champlain, is one of the most important waterways to the Adirondacks and this part of the new world.

And so the three most crucial and historically significant Adirondack waterways wear commemorative names: two, of their earliest visitors, Hudson and Champlain, and the third, of the name of the Saint whose calendar day marks the first landfall.

Immediately to the south of Lake Champlain lies that beautiful body of water visited quite early by the French and given the name, because of its beauty and purity, "La Lac du Sacrement," "the lake of the Sacrament." As you'll recall, this body of water maintained its lovely name till the final catastrophic decade, 1750–1760, the decade of what is called "The French and Indian War." And, as you remember, William Johnson chose to commemorate his king and renamed this lovely waterway "Lake George."

There is another exquisite lake on the east side of the Adirondacks. It too carries a commemorative name and its story is touching and wonderfully romantic, especially from a distance approaching four hundred years. It is a French name, although you'd never think so by seeing it in print or hearing it spoken. "Schroon Lake" is French in its heart, and its story is one of romance and chivalry. But let's wait till we look more closely at a whole cluster of French names in the Adirondacks.

Nor can we forget the name of a little lake on the edge of the small village of Saranac Lake. The little lake is not "Saranac Lake," however confusing that seems. No, the little body of water that graces the shore line of the village sports a commemorative name. When the dam that was to supply the village with electricity was built, it raised the level of the water in an area that had up to then been the shore line of a narrow stream, the outlet of the Saranac Lakes leading into the Saranac River. The then governor of New York was asked to lend his reputation, since he had already lent his support to the flooding of some lands in the Adirondack Forest Preserve in order to produce electric power. So on the occasion of the completion of the dam and the beginning of the age of electricity in Saranac Lake, the little artificial lake was called "Lake Flower," another of a number of commemorative names.

The vast majority of water names, to summarize, are personal and descriptive, and they tell of the presence of the common and ordinary people (mostly male) with ordinary and common names and ways of describing things. A few names remind us of events, some personal, others of historical importance. Some water names are of Native American origin and of Native American presence. Some water names hint at the movement of ethnic groups in the Adirondacks other than Native American and "Yankee" Anglo-Saxon. And we see a number of major bodies of water named in honor of those who explored them or played important roles in connection with those waterways.

But we do more in the Adirondacks than enjoy its waters. We admire its skyline. We hike its forested trails. We climb its lofty peaks. Yet for the early settlers, the peaks were nothing but obstacles. They isolated us. They made getting supplies a burdensome and time-consuming venture. They surely made for poor farming. No, respectable folk stayed out of the mountains and left them for the bear and panther and wolf . . . and fools. Especially them city fools with nothing better to do than climb up and then back down. Bringing nothing valuable either way. Just talk. Any man with any brains got on with his affairs and stayed out of the mountains.

So it was until the 1820s and '30s, pretty late in the discovery and settling game, really. For by that time almost all the waterways had been located, mapped, however roughly, and, of course, named. Not so the mountains! And that lateness is the clue to the kinds of names our High Peaks wear. Not common and ordinary personal names. A mere pittance of good Anglo-Saxon, "American" descriptive names. No French, no ethnic spice and flavor. Just a bit of lip service to Native American ghosts wandering the high peaks. In truth, nothing like the vitality and energy and movement of our waterways.

Our peaks were named later than our waters, and they were named more selfconsciously than our waters. To paraphrase from that excellent book, *Peaks and People of the Adirondacks* (p. 6), with two exceptions the names of the lofty peaks originated from the scientific explorers and writers who came to the Adirondacks between 1800 and 1837.

The names of the mountains of the Adirondack High Peaks owe their popularity and accessibility, for the most part, to the active and influential men and women of the Adirondack Mountain Club, and in particular to one of its fine leaders, Russell Carson. In addition to his many other contributions, Carson was the universally acknowledged historian of the High Peaks. Do read *Peaks and People*. It offers you a delightful excursion into the world of the climbers, the guides, and the first explorers of the High Peaks. You'll also be introduced to that wonderful group, the world-renowned Adirondack 46ers. And reading this fine book will carry you into the mountains themselves, including their names.

Let's scan 42 of these 46 High Peaks when we've separated them into personal and descriptive names.

Personal Names		Descriptive Names
Allen	Armstrong	Basin
Blake	Clinton	Big Slide
Colden	Colvin	Cascade
Dix	Donaldson	Cliff
East Dix	Emmons	Dial
Esther	Gray	Giant
Hough	McComb	Gothics
Marcy (also known as Tahawus)		Haystack
Nye	Phelps	Lower Wolf Jaw
Porter	Redfield	Nippletop
Seward	Seymour	Panther
South Dix	Street	Rocky Peak
Wright		Saddleback
		Skylight
		Sawteeth
		Tabletop
		Upper Wolf Jaw
		Whiteface

Of these 42 famous High Peaks, a good majority bear the names of important Adirondack personages. With these few exceptions (life seems to enjoy plaguing us with the "few exceptions"): two guides, famous in the Adirondacks for their skills and personalities (and connections with more "important" Adirondack personages), Bill Nye and Old Mountain Phelps, have left their names upon the High Peaks. And one young girl, apparently for her lack of mountain skill, had an elevation named in her honor. It appears that Esther decided to climb Whiteface, became lost, and ended the night sleeping in discomfort, to put a good face on it, atop a height near Whiteface Mountain. The conclusion was a happy uniting of the 16–year-old girl with her family and this newly climbed peak named in her honor, Mount Esther.

But with the ever-present "few exceptions" of these three names, we can see that one more than half of the names of these High Peaks are personal names reflecting the presence and influence of the scientists and writers who explored and visited the area in the 1800–to–1837 period and the influence of the political figures in the governor's office during the crucial years of our state's development.

The remainder of these 42 names of the High Peaks elevations are descriptive. And the descriptive word/names used to portray these elevations appear at first glance to be reasonably common, almost pedestrian, certainly less than romantically elevated. Just look at "Big Slide" or "Tabletop" or "Sawteeth," for example. But this is just at first glance. When we take a look at these High Peaks names in contrast with the names of the less prestigious heights in the Adirondacks, the scene looks a bit different, as we'll see in a moment.

There are four elevations of the "46" that are not personal or descriptive. One is French, a corruption of Saint Anthony. That gives us the name "Santanoni." The other three commemorate the memory of Native American dominance in the area, with the names "Algonquin," "Iroquois," and "Couchsachraga."

Given the generally unspoken but understood sense of the importance of these High Peaks, and given the very self-conscious air taken by a good many of the early writers and explorers of the High Peaks, it shouldn't come as a surprise that the names chosen for these elevations are different from the names chosen for the other heights in the Adirondacks. It's somewhat like the differences between the great and important waterways and the out-of-the-way ponds.

The other elevations in the Adirondacks, and there are some 800 named (more or less), bear out these differences. For one thing, the personal names bestowed upon these "lesser" peaks generally refer to "lesser" personages—that is, "lesser" only in terms of the history books. Secondly, often it is the given or first name that graces the mountain, and this always hints at informality and familiarity. For example, "Mt. Marcy" and "Donaldson Mountain" sound more remote and more detached from mere mortals like us than the comfortable and reassuring "Billy Mountain" and "Kays Hill."

Throughout the Adirondacks we can find the likes of "Abes Hill," "Long Sue," "Thomas Hill," "Stella Mountain," "Phoebe Mountain," "Eddy Mountain," "Kitty Cobble," "Nick Mountain," "Francis Hill," and "Mount Tom." These names bring with them a level of familiarity, and even happy domesticity, as Clinton County offers us a "Nancy Ryan Mountain" to compliment its "Larry Ryan Mountain," or is it the other way around? Not since "Elizabethtown" and "Willsboro" of the Gilliland family have we met another place-name marriage.

Even in the names which describe physical features, the High Peaks remain more rarified. It may be only subjective on my part, but consider this: nowhere in the High Peaks do we meet "Dibble Hollow" or "Peach Blow Hill." No, "Dial," "Giant," "Whiteface," "Gothics": they reflect a bit of grandeur (how "Nippletop" got in is beyond me). But closer to earth we find "Plank Bridge Hill," "Jug Mountain," "Doctor Hill," "Burnt Hill," innumerable "Bald Hills" and "Bald Mountains," "Buck Hills," the ever-present "Lost Mountain," and the wonderfully mysterious "Gizzle Ocean Mountain."

Like peering into a still lake, the names of our peaks and our ponds mirror us.

8

A Babble Of Names

Travelers are always awed by the majestic vistas in the Adirondacks. The High Peaks and woodland trails, the waterways and valleys, autumn's explosive colors, the pristine ache of a winter's dawn: they are visions which fill the soul. Yet there is another kind of fullness offered by the Adirondacks. There is the richness of language, a veritable "Babble" of languages. And this linguistic exuberance has enriched our landscape.

It is extraordinary to consider, for example, that within the Adirondack Park there are some *seven* distinct languages at work (and often very much at play) on the mountains and lakes and in the settlements and logging camps. Seven separate tongues! A "Babble" indeed, and quite awesome. It is a miracle it all doesn't come tumbling down around us as we move from "Irishtown" to "Loch Bonnie" along "Le Roux Road!" It's almost as difficult to travel that path linguistically as it is physically.

Yet we do it every day in the Adirondacks. And what's more, in the doing our traditions and history and sense of what we are come to life and help us remember who we are. Our mix of "old" languages helps make us into the "new" people called "Americans." And, as we've begun to see, it is in the names on our landscape that we find much of the "old" tongues and the "old countries." It is in these place-names that we sometimes know about the people who spoke those languages.

Since it was the Native American who came first to the

Adirondacks, let's first look more closely at these *Amerindian* names (that's the preferred term in academic circles these days). First of all, Native Americans in the Northeast, as well as in most sections of the United States, rarely, if ever, named a place after a person, what we call a personal or commemorative name. I think this refusal to stamp the land with a person's name reflects the Native American's notion of custodianship rather than ownership of the land. But that line of speculation is best left to others. Let us stick to names.

When we see the postmark "Pontiac, Michigan" or an "Osceola" or a "Tecumseh," we do recognize not only a "place" in our country but a famous "Indian" as well. If we stop to think of it for a minute, we'll know that the name was given to that settlement by Whites, not by Pontiac or Osceola or Tecumseh or their peoples. And nowhere in our Adirondacks will we find any names commemorating any Algonkian or Iroquois put there by Native Americans themselves.

We do have a "Sabattis," for the very popular guide of the 1810 period who was the son of Captain Peter Sabattis (he who figured in Sir John Johnson's legendary rescue from the clutches of winter at "Raquette Lake"). And we do have a "Sabael" (a name you'll remember from the iron works on Mount Marcy and the "natural dam"). But, again, these settlement names were given by Whites interested in commemorating these two Native Americans, not by Native Americans themselves.

Just as American Indian leaders were commemorated by Whites in the naming of our cities, many American landmarks, natural and manmade, have been given Native American names. But not always of people. These names are of tribes and nations, and in the Adirondacks, of a confederacy of nations, the Iroquois. The Big Apple was perhaps named after the Manahatins; Montauk and its famous point perhaps owe their name to the Montauks. So does the state of Dakota (with an "L," not "D") owe its name to a people. And the American list goes on and on. Here in the Adirondacks (in addition to "Adirondacks") we have already noted the mountains "Algonquin" and "Iroquois."

Rather than personal or commemorative names, Native Americans created descriptive identifications for some feature of the place or offered some narrative of an event that took place there. Thus Native American names, when "translated" back into words, offer some physical record of the place, such as color or shape, or some event such as where a crossing was made or where a battle was fought. And, as we've noticed in "Syracuse," the Native American name often violates our romantic expectations of our "noble savages." "Stink Hole" gives pause to idealized fictions of the "natural man."

Native American names were, as far as I can see, always translucent in that they functioned as readily understood words describing or locating a place. In fact, the description often did the locating, for very often the name would "translate" into "Place where. . . ." Such is the case throughout the Adirondacks. Remember "CHI-GON-DER-O-GA" or "TI," "the place where waters sing as they swiftly cascade over the rocks into the lake?" Or consider "Akwesasne," the lands of the Mohawk in Franklin County on the edge of the St. Lawrence River. "Akwesasne" is said to mean "place where the partridges drum," that is, the sounds of this game bird fluffing its wings just before flight.

This practice of naming a place by some physical characteristic or by some locating description or incident helps explain how Native Americans named their waterways (at least those in the Adirondacks). Never did a river receive a name for its entirety. No, rivers and streams were the recipients of many names for different parts, as if they were like all other living creatures. I think this reflects another aspect of the Native Americans' response to their world, so different from that of the Europeans.' But that too is a line of speculation best left to others. We'll stick to names.

What would happen is that one place on a river or stream would become the point at which a crossing could easily be made, or where a special type of plant grew or an extraordinary event took place. That spot or place on the river or stream would then be known by the descriptive or narrative name. But it often happened that other events and other descriptions evolved other points or places on that waterway. Then the river got another name. And we know of waterways that bore lots of different names, depending upon whom you were talking to and where on the river bank you were standing.

Just consider "Saranac" for a moment. We know that some believe it means "place where the sumac grows." Now, if this is

an accurate translation of "Saranac," we can see how the area of
a river that had an identifiable and certainly localized plant
became the basis for the name of the entire waterway. But the
sumac does not grow the length of the Saranac River, and we
know there are other names for this river.

So we have three things to remember about the way Native
Americans named things. For one, they didn't use personal or
commemorative names. Secondly, they did use lots of
descriptive and episodic names. And thirdly, their waterways
had as many names as was necessary to describe the important
things about them. Very different from the way Whites do it.

In addition to using personal and national names of Native
Americans, Whites became very interested in "things Indian"
(that is, only after managing to remove most of them). So in the
Adirondacks a number of places were given "Indian" names.
"Kiwassa" in Saranac Lake Village is one example of this fad. So
are "Oseetah" and "Kushaqua." "Onchiota" is another; in fact,
at an earlier time "Onchiota" referred to a body of water and
meant "rainbow." This "Indian" name was dropped by the
White settlers in favor of its English translation, and
"Onchiota" became "Rainbow Lake," a name it still uses. Some
fifty years (more or less) later, in the 1880s, a railroad stop was
built near Rainbow Lake, and when it was discovered that the
now fashionable "Indian" word for "rainbow" was "Onchiota,"
you guessed it! This new community built by the railroad was
named "Onchiota." This may sound like something out of *Catch
22*, but truth is stranger than. . . .

This spate of coining "Indian" names reached its peak in
the last two decades of the 1800s. As Beauchamp noted, with his
usual dry understatement:

> Many Indian names have been recently applied to camps
> and summer houses in the wilderness, as Cohasset,
> Manhasset, Mohawk and Onondaga camps, and Iroquois
> and Hiawatha lodges.

Beauchamp's *Aboriginal Place Names of New York,* from which
comes this observation and a good deal of the following
information about specific Native American names, is a
wonderful reference compiled from all other previous material
on Iroquoian and Algonkian names in the Adirondacks.

Published in the beginning of this century, it is the starting point
for anyone interested in Native American Adirondack names.

Our love affair with "things Indian" manifests itself in more
than Hollywood movies. Many of our states, and many of our
great lakes and rivers, such as Erie and Mississippi, many of our
national parks and forests, such as Yosemite, and many of our
great cities, such as Chicago and Miami and glorious Manhattan
of New York City, are blessed with "Indian" names. And in the
Adirondacks there are, in addition to the village, mountain and
water names of Native American origin, so many "Indian
Trails," "Indian Points," "Indian Rocks" that one would think
the area suffering from overpopulation and urban blight. In
truth, these "Indian" names perhaps reflect a White perception
of Native American presence more than anything else.

Given the myths and mysteries of "Indian" names, I think
it will be fun to look at some Native American names of a few
prominent places in the Adirondacks, places you might travel
through, if not to. And remember, it can be almost as much fun
to travel using just your map and finger, tracing all sorts of paths
through the Adirondacks. You can get to a lot of places quicker
(and cheaper) that way. But whether by car or by imagination,
when you get to an "Indian" name remember: it was put there by
Whites; it is descriptive and/or episodic, and generally not very
romantic in translation; and it refers to one point only on a river
or stream.

Moving north out of Albany, one sees the roadway sign
pointing to the community of Niskayuna. You couldn't tell at all
now, but the name "Niskayuna" comes from the descriptive
phrase, "field covered by corn," or "Connestigune." Since the
Mohawk were, indeed, an agricultural people, and maize was a
major crop, this seems reasonable, especially in the light of the
Native American name of the community that became "Half
Moon," not far at all from Niskayuna. Before it was renamed for
Hudson's exploratory ship it was called "Canistaguaha,"
"people of pounded corn."

Once truly on the Northway, I-87, you have to be very
careful not to allow your eyes to rest overly long on the sign
"Kayaderosseras." See, you're doing it now! It's an eyeful as well
as a mouthful. The sign (and name) refers to a mountain range
and district, and however musical it sounds (once you've worked

on it a bit), it translates into "lake country," although some favor "long deep hole." So much for what we know!

But once on to Saratoga we might expect more precision, more surety about its meaning. Not to be! "Saratoga" is as conjectural as "Kayaderosseras" (I only wrote it again because it's such a marvel). Listen to "Saratoga's" possibilities: "the sidehills," "salt springs," "place of sparkling waters," "place or people of swift waters," "where the prints of heels may be seen." Beauchamp dismisses all these "translations"; however, some seem to fit, hinting at what we know as folk etymology. To pick the right one would be like picking all the winners at next year's Saratoga racing season!

Well into the Adirondacks now, still on I-87, we come to one of the gems of the region, Schroon Lake. It is a place truly gemlike, but not if you care for its supposed "Indian" name. We're told it might be "Skanetaghrowahna," meaning "largest lake," or "Sknoonapus," loosely connected to "he pours out water." Whatever the ultimate verdict, neither "Sknoonapus" or "Skanetaghrowahna" pleases me. I much prefer the French contender, and I think you will also. But we'll hold off on that for a few minutes.

Somewhat farther north into Essex County, we'll meet a modest little elevation that gains enormous attention because of its name. If you need an illustration of the power in a name, here it is. You drive along on the Northway, Lake Champlain on your right, sometimes giving you a glimpse of her beauty, and the High Peaks on your left, sometimes clearly outlined, sometimes shrouded, but never with the special attention-getting character of our little Poke-O-Moonshine. What a strange name, "Poke-O-Moonshine." Must have something to do with the Prohibition Era, bootleg whiskey and home-grown booze and private "stills" back in the hills. But that isn't it at all. It's a "Indian" name and has nothing to do with "firewater." It comes from "pohqui," "it is broken," and "moosi," "smooth." Hence, "Pohquimoosi," "where the rocks are smoothly broken off." Not overly exotic, but not illegal either.

Were we to gaze beyond Poke-O-Moonshine into the High Peaks, we couldn't help but notice the king of all the elevations, "Tahawus." I could have said "Mt. Marcy," but many of us in the Adirondacks think of this highest of all New York State peaks as celebrating Native Americans, not governors.

And now we're passing the Saranac River again. Not "sumac" this time, but near its entrance into Lake Champlain. Perhaps the phrase "mouth of a river" is appropriate, since it is in Plattsburgh that the Saranac spills into the lake. And one Native American name for the Saranac River may be "S'nhalo'nek." Close enough, I think. But remember, this river carries a number of names.

There are two communities in St. Lawrence County with names that can instruct as well as delight: "Potsdam" and "Massena Springs." We've seen how some Native American names look and sound musical and romantic. Yet their meanings are often common and even worse. With "Potsdam," we have a case of not being able to decide which is less attractive, the Native American or the German name. With all respect to the good people of this fine community, their name is not one to take pleasure in. "Potsdam" sounds awful. The "Indian" name "Tewatenetarenies," although a mouthful, does offer musical relief from "Potsdam." But the meaning of "Tewatenetarenies?" "Place where the gravel settles under the feet in dragging the canoe." As I say, the unpleasantness of "Potsdam" is matched by the prosaic flatness of "Tewatenetarenies."

"Massena Springs," on the other hand, carries with it a hint of the classic as well as the prestigious. After all, "Springs" are the "Spas" where the rich and famous migrate periodically, and "Massena" is impressively Hellenic, if misspelled. Now, the Native American name appears quite stentorian, quite grand in its own way. Alas, we are to be reminded again of the sometimes ordinary vision of some of the early visitors to the Adirondacks. The "Indian" name "Kanaswastakeras" means "where the mud smells bad"! We're back at Syracuse!

If we're going to see quirks and bends in these names, we might just come back to the Oswegatchie River for a moment. It doesn't mean "I Gotch Ye," you'll recall, and it doesn't mean "going around a hill" either. That bit of folk etymology goes along with the capture scene, doesn't it? No, the meaning, we've seen, is much less dramatic: merely "black water."

Down in Hamilton County there is a famous lake and park, a magnificent summer camp created by Seward Webb. Webb, you remember, developed the railroad from Utica through the

Adirondacks and into Canada. He named his private park in the most romantic of ways, and the name "Nehasane" now refers to the park and the lake and the lodge and other camps and hotels and on and on. Despite its musicality, the name means merely "crossing on a stick of timber." A very pedestrian name, I think.

And since we're in Hamilton County we can enjoy our Raquette River and Lake. "Tanawadeh," meaning "swift water," is one name of the Raquette. Another is derived from "Tanawadeh;" "Nihanawate" is said to mean "rapid river." And "Nihawanate" supposedly means "noisy river," which brings us closer to our racket. But another authority, that is, an earlier writer, claims that the shape of a meadow at the mouth of this river appeared to the French as similar to—you guessed it— a snowshoe. Hence, the French term, "raquette."

Although Champlain is a French commemorative name, everything Native American names are not, let's go over to this grand lake and see its other names. They're fascinating . . . and they make some points. Lake Champlain is really "Caniaderiguarunte," "the mouth or door of the country," or perhaps it is "Petwo-pargow," "great water," or perhaps "Petaonbough," "lake branching into two," or "Petowahco," "entering a mountain," or "Caniaderi Oit," "tail of the lake," or "Andiatarocte," "the place where the lake contracts," or "Regioghne," "lake in which Rogeo drowned."

And there are other "Champlain" names of suggested Native American origin. The list does go on and on. What we can say is that definitive answers have not been given and perhaps never will be given. The mists of the past do make clear vision sometimes very, very difficult. But what we can also say is that all the suggested meanings and names point to the way Native Americans saw the landscape. They described their lands in terms of the physical traits of the landscape itself and in terms of incidents that mark their history on those landscapes.

I can't resist closing this section with a comment about one more name, this time from down in Washington County, a bit out of the North Country, but close enough. There is a little stream with the name of "Podunk Brook." It is said to derive from "Petunk," "to put into a bag," as well as other quite different possibilities. What I love about this Native American name is what it has come to mean as an American name. We have another "Podunk" in the Adirondacks, a "Podunk Road," but as one learns from one of our most respected authorities, Allen Walker Read (whom we'll meet again), people have sometimes called all of the Adirondacks "Podunk."

In many ways the explorations and early settlements of the French left as profound a legacy upon the names on the land as did the Native Americans. Often French names such as "Ausable" were descriptive, as were the Algonkian and Iroquoian. Again, as with Native American names, "Ausable" describes one point on the river, its estuary, and that point has become the descriptive name for the entire river. Just so with the Raquette River, of which we've made such a hue and cry.

But the French did indeed honor their great and named majestic parts of the New World with commemorative names: St. Lawrence, the great waterway; Lake Champlain, the great inland sea; and little Schroon Lake, the gem set in an edenic wilderness. But "Schroon" seems as French as "Potsdam" (and just as flat). Nevertheless, there is an old world courtliness, a touchingly romantic legend emanating from the most delicate of the French spirit that gives this explanation of this name's history the hope, if not the strength, of truth. It's a story we all love.

In the very early days, back when the English were looked upon by the Dutch, a/k/a Peter Stuyvesant, as newly arrived interlopers into the Big Apple, in these very early days . . . I feel like saying, "Once upon a time" . . . French explorers had already made themselves familiar with Lake Champlain and the areas on both sides of the lake in what are now Vermont and the foothills of the Adirondacks. One of the most beautiful of lakes discovered by these early French explorers was a body of water so pure in its essence and so perfect in its ambience that it called for a very special designation.

It so happened that at that time in Paris, the court of Louis XIII was celebrating the joining of a unique couple. All French nobility was admiring, gossiping about, buzzing around, conjecturing over a poet and a woman. The woman was a great beauty whose father had fallen out of favor with the king and who had been reduced to humiliating poverty. The poet was a nobleman, a wit, an intellectual, a magnet of conversation, a sharp-tongued satirist, a sensitive lyricist; in short, everything admired was to be found in him. He also was a deformed hunchback.

"Cyrano de Bergerac," the wonderful play and, in our time, a movie, of the exceptionally gifted and spirited nobleman with all the world at his feet . . . except that he loves the beautiful Roxanne and he is plagued with a grotesquely long nose . . . is the model for this real-life, tragic lover.

This poet and wit and nobleman of Louis' court, madly in love with the young beauty reduced to poverty, courted her despite his deformity. And she fell in love with his charm and sensibilities and courtly grace! They were united, with Louis' blessing, and became the lions of the social season at Louis' court (that she eventually became one of Louis' mistresses is of no account here). The "chevaliers" of New France, the "Avacal," saw the romantic vision of the brilliant hunchback wedded to the beauty, giving her his name, Skaroon. In celebration of her beauty and virtue, and the triumph of love over all else, the new men of France in the new world called the lake of such exquisite purity and beauty "Lac du Skaroon."

Unlike "Lac du Sacrement," which Sir William Johnson renamed "Lake George," "Lac du Skaroon" experienced no major confrontations during the years of English and French hostility. And the transfer of power from French to English hands in the Adirondacks did not affect "Lac Skaroon" in terms of its name, other than to see it pronounced differently. The English often do not care for French ways (except when it suits them) or French pronunciations (except when they want to impress), and so as the years moved on the English and then the Americans saw not "Skaroon," which rhymes with "lagoon," but ultimately "Schroon," which rhymes with . . . nothing. Such is the guttural ending to a romantic and exotically French love story and name.

Many other French names remained in the North Country after the French themselves were removed by the English and their Iroquoian allies. There are township names such as "DePeyster," "Louisville" and "Pierrepont," as well as village names like "DeGrasse." We won't find the likes of a Lake Champlain everywhere, but throughout the Adirondacks, especially in the northern and eastern sections, we will run across a "Corbeau Creek," a "Le Goys Brook," a "Guay Creek," even a "Lake Chartreuse!" And let's not forget our "Lamora Mountain," "Lesperance Mountain," and "Frenette Mountain." And one gets to these places often by taking the "French Settlement Road."

A second wave of names of French origin came to the Adirondacks some forty years after the French left in 1760. This is the period described so well by Edith Pilcher in her *Castorland,* the story of the French nobility who attempted to escape the 1792 revolution and create a new empire in the Adirondacks. And "Castorland" remained as a stop for the New York Central Railroad till the 1930s, over one hundred years later. It translates, as you know, as "land of the beaver," a cousin to the "Antient Couchsachrage."

"Lake Bonaparte" remains as one of the more intriguing stories of this misadventure by the French. Joseph Bonaparte felt the end of his brother's reign in the cards and, before meeting his own Waterloo, left for Philadelphia's Main Line. We're a very democratic people, but we do love our royalty, especially when they're foreign! So Philadelphia society took Napoleon's brother to its bosom in 1815 as the Comte De Survilliers. Joseph, after many whirls of the social sets, acquired some Adirondack property from one major proprietor of the Castorland tract, James LeRay, in addition to establishing his mistress and daughter in Watertown, Joseph found much solace for the loss of his Spanish throne in hunting on the expanse of land he had purchased. There are wonderful stories of Bonaparte entertaining his Philadelphia friends with picnics in the wilds, lunching on Limoge china whilst "native" guides stalked the perimeters keeping a lookout for wolves! At any rate, Joseph left his name on the lake near his manor house, and his love of hunting induced him to name the township "Diana."

In addition to full-bodied French names, the Adirondacks enjoys using the French term for settlement or village, "ville," in combination with English names and words. So the French "ville" joins with William Keese in producing the name of the community "Keeseville." It does sound better than "Keese-burgh," doesn't it?

A last wave of French swept into the Adirondacks after the Civil War, when the post-war boom in the Northeast called for vast amounts of timber for the building of houses and factories. And the Adirondacks became the major supplier of timber to the East Coast markets. The call went out and French-Canadians came into the woods to cut and drive the logs to the mills. And this period, 1870 to 1900, saw the emerging of pockets of settlements known as "Frenchtown," or "French Hill," or "French's Hollow," and often you got there on "French Road!"

Some of these roads illustrate in the most humorous way how the mix of languages can produce names absolutely new in the world, names not possible unless the languages mix and breed and produce these lovely offspring. Nowhere but in this new world could you find a "La Rue Road!" How about "La Flesh Road?" Or try "La Duke Road." Or "Le Bridge Road." And a little later on we'll hear echoes of our Cajun friends on "Phelix Road."

To the Algonkian, Iroquoian and French names on the Adirondack landscape are added a few Dutch and Scottish names. Remember, Dutch names remain primarily in the New York City area, the Catskill region ("Catskill" itself is a Dutch name), the Hudson Valley below Albany, and in a few places north of Albany on the way into the Adirondacks.

There is "Half Moon." There is "Watervliet," another community nearby, which you'll know most probably by the signs on I-87 as you head north. See how the Dutch "vliet" has been joined with the English "water," as the translation from Dutch to English was only half finished.

The most familiar of Dutch names for most of us are connected not with the Bronx or Yonkers or even Broadway and Coney Island, although these names all are good Dutch words. No, the Dutch most recognized by us is the ending "kill." And the meaning, "fast moving stream or brook," gave rise to one of my most exciting, if disappointing, detective hunts.

Back in the early 1970s, one of my students collected a list of names of older settlements along the Saranac River between Plattsburgh and Vermontville, roughly following Route 3. A large section of this area had been called "New Sweden" at an earlier time because of the richness of the deposits of iron found liberally throughout the countryside. In fact, "Keeseville" at one time had been called "Birmingham," after the great industrial

English city. The confluence of water power, fuel and iron deposits suggested the growth of a major iron and steel industrial center. And the village of Dannemora, on the edge of this "New Sweden," took its name for a particularly fine strain of Swedish ore.

Given all this, you will understand my excitement about the list of names of settlements along the Saranac River section of "New Sweden" when you hear that there was a lot of repetition of the term "kill." It was certainly clear to me. My reputation as an Adirondack historian was assured. Despite the accepted historical view that early Dutch influences extended only so far as a bit north and west of Albany, I now had explosively contradictory evidence. "Kill" meant Dutch influence, and repeated "kills" along a body of swiftly running water could mean only one thing. The Dutch had been here! They had established early settlements, named their places, and, despite moving on or being forced out, had managed to leave behind their language in these settlement names.

Can you fault me my arrogant excitement, my youthfully pretentious superiority? I had recognized an historic period or at least an episode completely overlooked by every student of the Adirondacks and Champlain Valley, not to speak of the giants of New York State history. Visions of Academic Applause danced in my head! And I began to write The Monograph that was to shake the historical world.

First I listed a sampling of "Dutch" names: "Smith Kill Brook" in Clinton County and "Copper Kill Pond" in Essex County. I assumed the Dutch term "kill" followed by a water "generic," brook or pond, represented just one more set of examples of the word "kill" losing its meaning as a word and living on as a name.

Farther south in Warren County one finds "Dippikill Pond" and "Dippikill Mountain" and "Kattskill Bay," among others with the "kill" ending. Washington County offered up as evidence for The Monograph such names as "Batten Kill" and "Moses Kill." I was hot on the trail of a direct path from the heart of Dutch activity in Albany (Beverwyk, to them) to the "kills" along the Saranac.

Now Saratoga threw me off the trail for a bit by its refusal to cooperate and turn over any evidence of "kills." But when you're

determined to want things a certain way, you see what you want
to see. Don't we! So I saw, if not "kills," lots of "vlys:" just about
A to Z, "Archer Vly" to "Vly Creek." Now "vly" is a Dutch word
for swamp, and so I would use this evidence to shore up The
Monograph. The trail was a bit confused, but we could still
march along on it, I thought.

But, back in the High Peaks we located . . . "Kiln Brook!"
This was still in the early stages of The Monograph, and I was
brought jarringly to earth. A closer look at some early maps of
the "New Sweden" region disclosed the suffix "kill," sure
enough, but also more evidence of "kilns." And my theory of
Dutch presence went up in smoke, if you'll forgive the pun, from
those kilns.

What occurred, it is clear enough, was a common problem
for anyone trying to write down names. As sounds become
translated into written words, the spelling of these words
sometimes changes the meaning. Although not exactly the
same, the Cajun tale explains it pretty well. According to the
story, this old Cajun, a weathered, old Louisiana bayou hunter
whose roots went back to French-Canadian Quebec, lost his
faithful hunting dog and ran an advertisement in the newspaper
giving the dog's name as Phydeaux. No one had ever heard of
such a name for a dog and the old Cajun didn't see Phydeaux
again till the notice was given to the local radio. It was
announced (and pronounced), calling for information about a
missing hunting dog who answered to the name Fido. Just like
"Phelix Road!"

And just so with "kills." The iron foundries had insatiable
appetites for fuel in order to render the ore into iron. Thus the
early days saw innumerable stands of hardwood trees such as
oak and beech cut and delivered to innumerable furnaces, which
slowly burned the logs into charcoal. These charcoal-making
furnaces were really much more like ovens—sometimes they
were merely massive holes in the ground covered with dampened
leaves and mosses—and surely functioned like pottery ovens or
kilns. The entire area was dotted with these kilns, and the names
of settlements as well as these "ovens" took on the suffix "kiln"
with whatever name came before it.

But, as in Phydeaux, the distance between the spelling and
the saying causes much confusion. "Kiln" (pronounced "kill"

without the final 'n') was written as it sounded, and the Dutch word describing water was written for what was meant to be the potter's oven, a kiln. Nowadays, by the way, I've heard the oven pronounced with the final 'n'; this is a great improvement, I think. At any rate, my "Dutch Theory" came to naught, fortunately before I had made a public statement in The Monograph.

Like the Dutch, Scottish influence remained very much out of the Adirondacks, with the few exceptions here and there. We've seen "Loch Bonnie" in Essex County, representing a hint of Scottish presence in the High Peaks or reflecting someone's romantic familiarity with Scotland. And, of course, the spelling of "Plattsburgh," with its Scottish suffix, also suggests the hint of the Highlanders in the North Country.

One finds in Lake George "Scotch Bonnet" island and nearby the village of "Glenburnie." North of that near Schroon Lake is the village of "Loch Mueller." There is a post office nearby, spelled "Loch Muller." The evolution moves toward completion and total "Americanization" on the "Lock Miller Road." One can enjoy a "Scotch Lake" in Hamilton County, although one may wonder (from a distance) whether this reflects ethnic or alcoholic preference. In St. Lawrence County, "Scotch Settlement Road" is less equivocal.

These Scottish names comprise a very limited number in terms of all the names decorating the Adirondack landscape. Let us be cautioned by my "kill" misadventure and not see Scots where they are not.

I think we might also note "Mt. Van Hoevenberg," near Lake Placid. Not Scottish, of course, but an honored example of a commemorative name of one of German ancestry, significant in the development of winter sports in the High Peaks, especially in what has come to be called (if only by public relations people) "The Olympic Region."

With the inclusion of these few Dutch, Scottish and Germanic names to the French, Algonkian and Iroquoian Nations, we can see the short of babble of names characteristic of the Adirondacks. And when we add the names made up of the mixes of all these languages, . . . well, we are an amazing country, aren't we? But always, the one language that unites us all, the language that gives us most of our names and helps us know where we are in the Adirondacks, is English.

The type of English name, of course, varies, as we have seen: descriptive, commemorative, personal, episodic, transfer, and fanciful. And on occasion, as we have also seen, the English name is a translation or transliteration of a Native American name, such as "Ticonderoga," or a repronunciation of a French name, such as "Ausable" and, if you prefer that story, "Schroon," or a combination of Dutch and English, as in "Watervliet." But whatever the mix, these names have become part of our language of names; they are English names.

Along with the variety of types and combinations of names, the sheer number is astounding. In an area blessed by 2½ million (more or less) acres in which the Constitution of New York State forbids development under our "Forever Wild" provision, in this area historically bypassed in the search for lands to farm and settle and populate, in this "Northern Wilderness," there are, nevertheless, some 30,000 (more or less) separate names recorded by the United States Board of Geographic Names. And we know that the number of names not recorded, the hidden "Frog Hollows," the narrow sideroad names, the informal local names, the village street names, all these names in the Adirondacks add up to a great deal more than 30,000. And, of course, most of these are English names.

Let's look at one English name in the Fulton Chain, near First Lake. It's an interesting example of the how and why of some names and the kinds of pressures that create the history of a name. The place is now officially marked as "Rondaxe Mountain," and you'll note that it sits overlooking First Lake.

Some hundred and twenty-five years ago, a native of the Adirondacks, Benjamin Stickney, who had moved west to St. Louis, became very wealthy manufacturing rifles for the Union army in the Civil War. Although he was now part of St. Louis' social elite, it is impossible to take the Adirondacks out of a person even if you take the person out of the Adirondacks, to paraphrase a fine Americanism.

Stickney returned to the Adirondacks and First Lake (at least for the summers) around 1866, and had himself built— some ten years before it became fashionable among the Very Rich—a "Camp." The "Camp" consisted of a main house, guest cottages, servants' quarters, et. al. It was, indeed, an early hint of the opulence to be exhibited by the Vanderbilts and Rockefellers and Posts in their "Camps" in the Adirondacks of the 1880s.

Stickney enjoyed his summer retreat and introduced to the Adirondacks many of his St. Louis friends. They were so delighted with the beauty of the region that within the next decade a colony of St. Louis families could be found on the lakes of the Fulton Chain. And with this colony, this "critical mass" of people, as today's social scientists term it, came a certain degree of tension between the locals and the wealthy outsiders.

Sometimes this tension was reduced and happy accommodations were made, such as with the Webbs at Nehasane. At other times, such as with the tragedy of Orlando Dexter, the tensions became so unbearable and the communication became so hostile that in 1903 Mr. Dexter was shot and killed by "persons unknown." But nothing of this sort emerged at First and Second Lakes. The battle between locals and outsiders was limited, as far as I can tell, to a confrontation over a name, an "onomastic war," if you will.

An elevation that has looked down upon the beauty of the waters of First and Second Lakes for millennia had been named by the early explorers and settlers of the area. What, if any, name was used by Native Americans is unknown to me. But we do know that our predecessors looked upon the height, noticed its special features and called it "Bald Mountain." Perhaps not the most poetic of names, but a time-honored description that suited the vision of these early Adirondackers.

The summer gentry, however, bringing to the wilds of the Adirondacks the best of St. Louis sensibilities and culture, felt that "Bald Mountain" was too . . . how shall we put it . . . too common a name. Especially if, when entertaining guests, one were to be questioned concerning the name of that mountain overlooking one's summer hideaway. "Bald Mountain" would not do as an address, nor would it do as a conversation piece in mixed company. "Bald Mountain" would not do.

In order, therefore, to eliminate the stigma of such an impossible name—no matter how democratic a nation we are— and in order to bring a little bit of home with them in their summer hideaways, the "Gentry of First and Second Lakes" renamed the mountain! Yes they did! No longer were we in the

shadow of "Bald Mountain;" we could now revel in the majesty
of "Mt. St. Louis!" And in the informal way wealth and position
could manage things in the 1880s, these St. Louis colonists in the
Adirondacks were able to get official maps changed and their
choice of name used with formal documents. "Mt. St. Louis" it
was to be! The common, democratic, people's vividly unpreten-
tious and earthy descriptive name gave way to . . . "Mt. St.
Louis," a foreign transfer name. Or so were the best laid
plans.

In 1066 A.D. when the Normans took over in Britain, they
brought with them French as the official language of the British
Isles. And the natives went on in their own way speaking good
old Anglo-Saxon. It took a mere 300 years for the conquered to
conquer, and French succumbed completely to the glory of
Chaucer's earthily sublime English. Oh yes, some French
survived and came in and enriched the possibilities of our
language, but it is the glory of English to absorb the foreign, the
pretentious, the superficial cosmopolitanism, and render vision
and thought and feeling into language that touches the souls of
all of us.

And as the English yeoman (or yeoperson) went on dealing
with his or her world in good old Anglo-Saxon, the Adirondacker
went on dealing with Bald Mountain as Bald Mountain. So it
went. "Mt. St. Louis" to some, Bald Mountain to others. And
never the twain shall meet.

In an attempt to achieve a lasting peace, the government
stepped in and decided to end the controversy by declaring a new
name to the elevation in question. Since a fire tower had been
installed atop "Bald St. Louis Mountain" (my suggestion for the
mediation table), and conservation officials needed to refer to
the tower without disturbing the sensibilities of either group, the
peak was renamed "Rondaxe Mountain," a reference to and
contraction, of course, of "Adirondacks." Thus the descriptive
"Bald" became the transfer "St. Louis" became the commemorative contraction "Rondaxe."

But the last word has not been said, certainly not by the
government and certainly not by me. As I'm sure you've figured
out already, the good people of the Fulton Chain, our
Adirondack yeopeople, mark the height not of government fiat
or of affluent power, but of Bald Mountain.

English laced with French; English and French spiced with Iroquoian and Algonkian sounds; English, French, Iroquoian and Algonkian, with sprinklings of Dutch, Scottish and German; a wonderfully rich mix of languages and names, equal to the rich mix of people who make up our land.

9

A Pond By Any Other Name

We are an extraordinary phenomenon. We humans are as partial to contradictions as we are devoted to logic. It's as if we insist upon the freedom to break rules, upon the right to establish our own multi-faceted enigmas. To what else can we attribute the Sixth Name Law, alias No Ditto? Let me explain.

As we've seen, names serve to establish a distinction, a uniqueness about a place. The name separates that place from its surroundings as it locates and describes, commemorates or identifies. And, as many have also observed, to name a place is to humanize it, to domesticate it. Were we to wax philosophic, we might speculate along with the Existentialists that to bestow a name is to create "being" where none was. But let's not wander too far into the realm of "meaning of meaning." Let's remain firmly on the ground in the Adirondacks. It's enough for us to say that naming a place gives it an identity and a location that distinguishes it from its surroundings. The name separates the place from its surroundings. Now, that's good, basic, common sense.

Let's digress a moment and talk about personal names, the names we people take, to underscore the truth of this "Non-Ditto Law," this Sixth Law of Names. Until the late Middle Ages, around the fourteenth century (more or less), the Western world got along quite nicely without "family" names; that is, what we call "sir names," that is, "surnames" or "last names." To be sure, nobility did enjoy titles and some took "last names," but the rest of us—which included almost all of us—did just fine with a straightforward "Anne" or "John" or "Mary" or "Robert."After all, in a world sparsely populated, there were enough names to go around without causing any confusion.

But then there was a population explosion, and one day we woke up to find in our small village six "Annes," twelve "Johns," fourteen "Marys" and seven "Roberts." Obviously this wouldn't do, except for a Shakespearean farce, and so we hit upon the expedient of a "second name," a "surname," a "last name," a "family name."

With that, the "Annes" became different "Anne Somebodies," as did the "Johns," "Marys" and "Roberts" of the world. How and why they hit upon the "second" name is another, and fascinating, story. But that's for a different book. What is important for us is the lesson this little bit of personal name history teaches. When a name is duplicated too often, it will create confusion rather than produce clarity.

In a village with fourteen "Marys," twelve "Johns," seven "Roberts" and six "Annes," for a start, we're better off with no names at all! Thus, we have in operation the Sixth Name Law: another name is necessary when one name is used over and over again. Now that's just good, common sense! And it's as true for places as it is for people.

George R. Stewart's wonderful narrative of American place-naming, *Names On The Land* (pp. 240–241), touches on this point:

> In colonial times the central authority . . . had controlled the naming of towns, and duplications within a colony had been unknown. But with the Revolution every man was as good as another to give a name . . . under the banner of democracy arose an unfortunate repetition of the more popular names. . . .
>
> In New York . . . the situation became bad enough to goad the Legislature into action. On April 6, 1808, a resolution was passed: 'Whereas considerable inconvenience results from several of the towns in the state having the same name. . . .' Thereupon the Legislature without further regard for local feelings changed the names of thirty-three places.

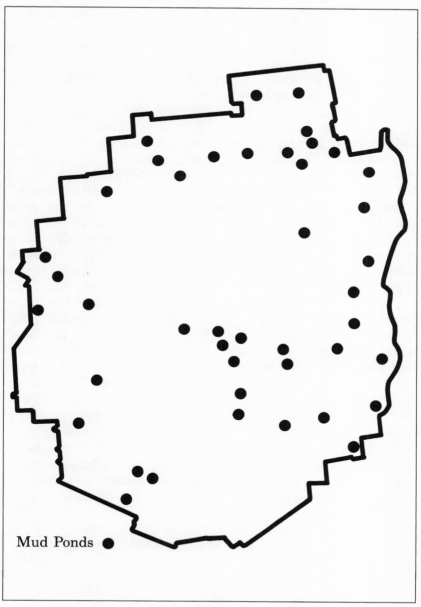

Mud Pond: All 43

There appears to be one exception to this rule (always the exception!) for place names, and that is when we consider "Transfer" names. You'll recall, the motive for that kind of name is to help create a likeness or at the least to rekindle a memory of another place in the past. With a transferred name, the *function* is to identify and locate and make separate a place, but the *motivation,* at least covertly, is to duplicate, if only for memory's sake, a former home or landscape.

Even then the Sixth Name Law works, because we often give places a "second" name, as if they were like our "Johns" and "Marys." We refer to our national capital not simply as "Washington" but more formally as "Washington, D. C." And "Athens" takes the "surname" "Georgia" as well as "Ohio." "Plymouth" is known as Plymouth, Massachusetts or Plymouth, Connecticut or Plymouth, Pennsylvania or Plymouth, Indiana, to name only the closest relatives. And there is quite a difference in how one dresses when visiting Miami if her last name is "Ohio" rather than "Florida." Imagine a state with thirty "Troys" in it. No wonder they all need "last" names.

When the using of the state in which the name lives as a "surname" was not feasible, we could, and did, create a "pre" name. We introduced our place by calling it "New." That way nobody would mix up England with New England, or York with New York. Or we used the compass for our "pre" name. "North" and "South" separate the "Dakotas," and "West Virginia" is not "Virginia." So whether it be by using a "pre" name or a "last" name, we were able to transfer our names.

With the exception of "transfer" names, then, we expect names to be different from each other. Or to put it into more formal, if not clearer, language, the degree of efficient use of names is diminished in proportion to the degree of duplication practiced. This law is a necessary preamble to our Sixth Name Law, No Ditto.

Well then, in an area the size of the Adirondacks, which for all its diversity does boast a common heritage of mountains, waterways, climate and plant and animal life, we do have a right to expect enough different names so that we know where we are, where we're going, and whom and what to expect when we get there. And by and large this is so. After all, our maps are reasonably clear and certainly helpful as we traverse the North

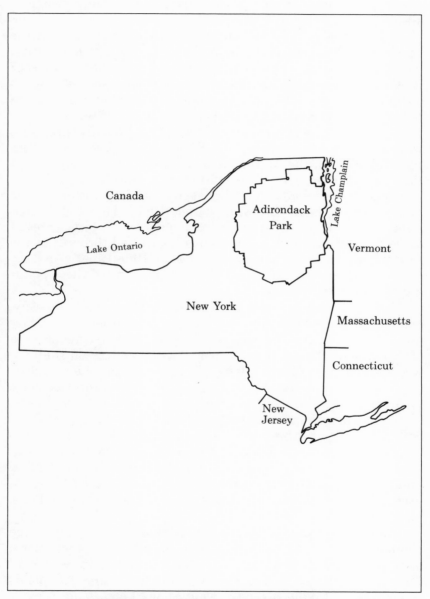

The Adirondacks in Relationship to
the Rest of New York State

Country. It does seem that humankind is logical and consistent, after all.

Nevertheless . . . but there it is again, the orneriness of the human psyche emerges, and in the midst of all this clarity, pattern, logic and consistency in name usage, what do we see? By God! There it is again . . . we break the pattern. We thumb our noses at logic; we create . . . out of sheer devilishness, I'm tempted to believe . . . the "Phenomenon of Ditto."

We look for a good fishing hole called "Mud Pond," and what do we find? FORTY-THREE of them! Yes, forty-three "Mud Ponds" in the Adirondacks. Now let me assure you that the waters of these ponds are not dirty or muddy at all. They are usually clear and delightful. It's just that the dark bottoms of the ponds tend to make the water appear dark. Hence, "Muddy Pond." Now consider this amazing phenomenon: forty-three of these delightfully clear "Mud Ponds" scattered throughout the Adirondacks within the confines of the "Blue Line." And the schematic map (see page 121) shows that many of these ponds are pretty close to each other!

This interesting name, "The Blue Line," by the way, emerged in 1890 when the State of New York drew a boundary around the Forest Preserve to establish the perimeter of a contemplated State Park (see page 123). The line on the map was indeed drawn in blue ink to distinguish it from the boundary of the Forest Preserve. Hence the term, Blue Line (see page 125).

Now back to our "Mud Ponds," all forty-three of them. I contend that forty-three repeats of a pond name in an area the size of the Adirondack Park is pretty ornery, in anybody's book. But consider this: sixteen pond names are repeated two hundred and twenty-nine times! Even more, twelve names for lakes are used eighty-four times! And nineteen mountains share only six names!

If that doesn't call for serious head-shaking over the contemplation of this mass confusion, consider these repetitions: sixteen "Clear Ponds" (five of them right next to "Mud Ponds!"); fourteen "Lost Ponds" (strange name for ponds discovered and rediscovered); twenty-one "Long Ponds;" eight "Long Lakes" (lots of these "Long Ponds" are larger and longer than many of the "Long Lakes"); sixteen "Round Ponds;"

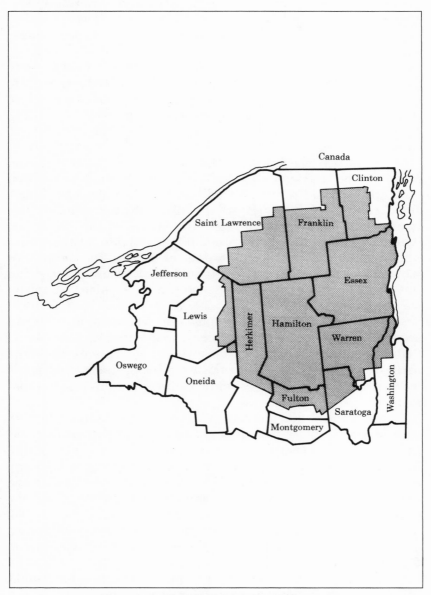

Close-Up of the North Country and
the Adirondack Park Blue Line

fourteen "Rock Ponds;" thirteen "Grass Ponds;" ten "Lily Pad Ponds;" seven "Cranberry Ponds;" fourteen "Deer Ponds;" twelve "Buck Ponds;" ten "Bear Ponds;" and nine "Beaver Ponds."

We are in the land of the "Ditto-Name!" Is there any possibility of explanation aside from putting this down to mere human perversity? Let's take a look at our schematic illustrations of some of these name repetitions within the Blue Line. Perhaps there are some clues in where these ponds are located. (see pages 127–130)

For the rest, the fourteen "Rock Ponds," the sixteen "Round Ponds," the thirteen "Grass," the six "Pine," the seven "Cranberry," and ten "Lily Pad" ponds; the fourteen "Deer," the twelve "Buck," ten "Bear" and nine "Beaver" Ponds, I can assure you that schematic map illustrations of their locations will only serve to create profound eye strain, rather than understanding. The series of dots or circles or squares, or whatever designations are used to indicate locations, do nothing but reinforce the sense of happenstance, of accident, of topsy-turvy naming.

Three possible explanations for these amazing and seemingly haphazard duplications come to mind. First is the "No Imagination" charge. This theory postulates that the earliest people who came to the wilderness and named these waters were somehow devoid of imagination and verbal skills.

Besides the undemocratic bias to such a notion, the "No Imagination" theory just doesn't stand up to the evidence. If these hardy pioneers and settlers could leave us such a rich legacy of names as "Botheration Pond" and "Tight Nipping" and "Gizzle Ocean Mountain," to mention just a few, the charge of dullness of mind and tongue sputters out and dies. No, our predecessors were capable of name-giving that in many ways was richer, more imaginative, certainly less inhibited than those generally bestowed today. The "No Imagination" theory can be dismissed with no more time spent on it.

Another possibility is the "Translation" theory. One could understand the duplication of lake and pond names (and to a lesser extent mountain names) if it came about because places were named in more than one language. For example, suppose

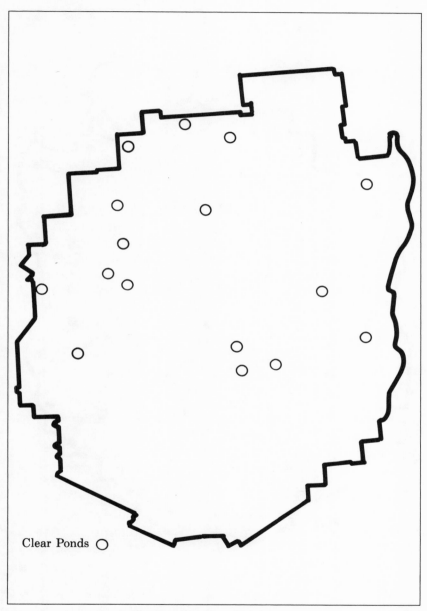

Clear Ponds ○

The 16 Clear Ponds

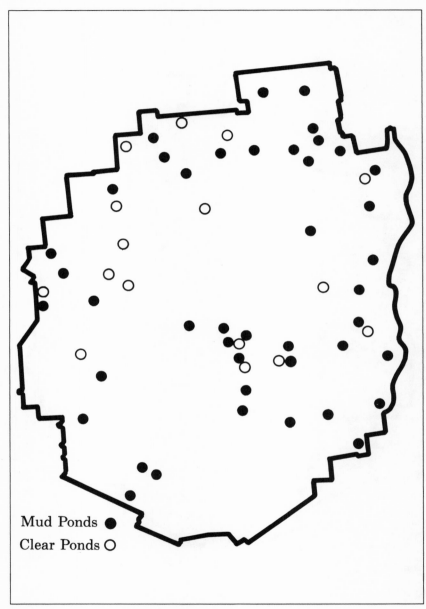

Mud Ponds and Clear Ponds

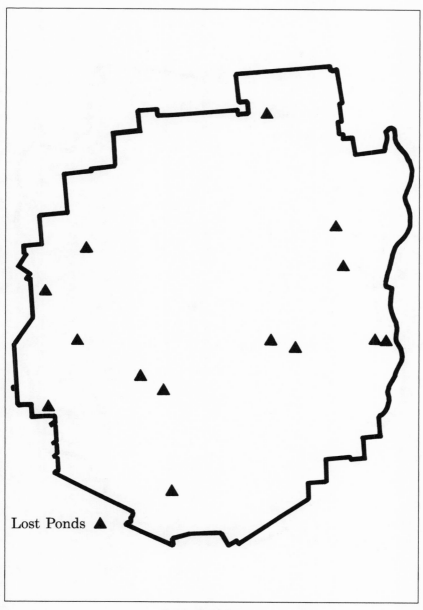

Lost Ponds ▲

Lost Ponds: 14

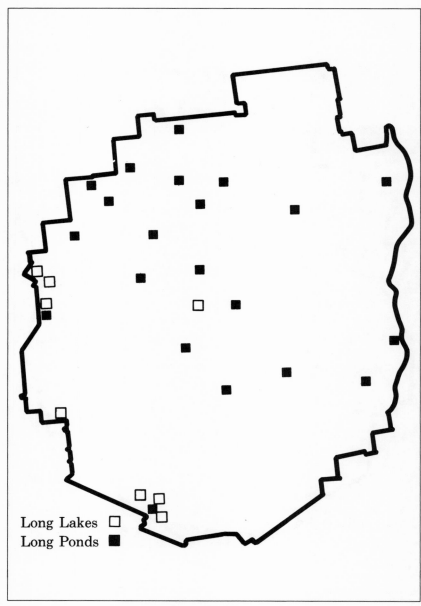

Long Ponds: (21) and Long Lakes: (8)

some French settlers had called a little body of water "Lac du Castor." Now suppose another group of settlers or explorers came across another body of water in the general vicinity and called it "Beaver Pond." You'd then have a "Lac du Castor" and a "Beaver Pond" in the same neighborhood, and there would be no problem telling one from the other by its name.

But suppose the French settlers were forced out of the area or just moved on to new places and a later generation of English-speaking people moved in. And suppose they preferred to translate their "Lac du Castor" into an English name. You'd have "Lake Beaver." Now English names tend to put the descriptive term before the general or "generic" term, unless it's a major waterway like "Lake Champlain" or "Lake George." So "Lake Beaver" would become "Beaver Lake." But if it were a little body of water, it would probably end up as "Beaver Pond," another "Beaver Pond."

Well, this sounds like a pretty good theory, even if somewhat fictional. But then again, there's many a theory that seems like fiction. In this case the fiction droops a little too heavy because the facts again don't seem to support the theory. We've seen so many French names absorbed into our maps and landscape, not by being translated as much as by being repronounced. We know the "Ausable" not as "to the sands" but as "Awe Say Bull," with the stress on the middle sound. No, the multi-language layers of names in the Adirondacks did not produce forty-three "Mud Ponds."

There is just one other possibility that comes to mind: the "Migration" theory. As woodsmen, farmers, artisans, miners and lumbermen filtered into the Adirondacks from 1630 to 1830, they used three different routes, for the most part. Some came directly across Lake Champlain, generally the narrows at either the southern or northern ends; others moved west on the Mohawk River or through the Mohawk Valley until they turned northward at Fort Schuyler, a/k/a Utica, into the Adirondacks; a third group went north from or on Lake Champlain into the St. Lawrence River and then south and west, upstream, to the northern edges of St. Lawrence and Franklin Counties. These three routes were the main gateways to the Adirondacks.

Was it possible that the woodsmen and settlers in the heart of the remote and isolated forests identified and named places as if there were no others coming from other places? Is it possible, for example, that settlers called a place "Lily Pad Pond," not knowing that another group of pioneers had settled some miles away and had named another body of water "Lily Pad Pond?" Is it possible that the broken terrain, the elevated passes, the difficulty of travel in a world without automobiles and snowmobiles, created pockets of settlers naming places independently of each other and unaware of each other's proximity? And because much of the Adirondacks does boast the same sort of plants and trees and animals and land and water, is it not possible that these descriptive names are merely accurate descriptions whose accuracy, however ironically, causes the confusing repetition?

Perhaps the characteristics of the landscape encouraged a kind of separateness of sections within the Adirondacks. And perhaps this separateness, geologically based, complemented the separate directions from which settlers came and reinforced the separateness of the pockets of settlements and names.

Could we not trace through place names pockets of settlements, separate colonies of settlers? And if so, could we not offer to the social historian a clue to the sometimes provincial, sometimes anachronistic, but always fiercely independent quality of the Adirondacker?

On the other hand, this last possibility, this "Migration" theory, might prove as ephemeral as the first two theories, as ephemeral as the Dutch settlements on the Saranac River! Till we know more, I'm content to rely upon the wisdom of a kind friend and wonderful teacher, Allen Walker Read. Called by H. L. Mencken (in 1948) the man who "probably knows more about early Americanisms than anyone else on earth," Professor Read's advice is worth heeding. Do not (I'm paraphrasing him), do not try to impose patterns where none seem to exist, merely for the sake of neatness. Be content with the pleasures of the variety and richness and sometimes orneriness of the American spirit.

10

That's No Fit Name For A Name

[ECCENTRIC], Possible synonyms: 1, off the wall; 2, flaky; 3, weird; 4, out of sight; 5, wow!; 6, awesome; 7, verrry interrrresting; 8, unreal, man; 9, and on and on. We are now in the realm of the Seventh Name Law, alias One man's meat. Now, first some awesome, heavy duty, serious theory!

Let's begin with the notion that what may be peculiar and idiosyncratic to one person may be perfectly acceptable, even if not absolutely common and ordinary, to another. So that what makes one person do a "double take" may seem to another person well within the realm of acceptability. This is RELATIVITY with a vengeance!

You might, for example, take a drive to "Paradox Lake" and spend the day enjoying the serenity with which this waterway is blessed. That this lake's calmness belies its name might not even enter your thoughts. You might not even think of the strangeness of such a name; you might not even think about the name at all (which would vouch for its onomastic validity). After all, we've just driven here to spend a nice day on the shores of "Paradox Lake." What's the big deal?

On the other hand, you might think it a very strange name indeed, and wonder about it, feeling it somehow to be a "peculiar" name, an "eccentric" name, an "odd" name for such a beautiful lake. Such a name, then, might be considered "eccentric" or "ordinary," depending upon the person contemplating it. This is one side of the "One Man's Meat Name Law."

The other side of the coin shows us ample evidence that what was ordinary for one generation becomes strange to another. So that despite some degree of individual preference, by and large the majority of people of any generation agree on what is eccentric and what isn't.

Consider 19th century "bathing costumes," for both men and women, which seemed to be designed to cover every inch of human skin with the exception of fingers and toes. Contrast this to our present G-String outfits, for both men and women! Surely someone sporting a Victorian beach costume at Malibu, circa 1990, would elicit extraordinary interest, stares and comment (might even be thought sexy!). And we can guess where some budding starlet (from Malibu, of course) would end up were she to have posed in her G-string for an 1890 Victorian beach scene!

So do times and customs and costumes change. And in names as well.

Imagine a modern, financier-type John Brown of Providence, a real estate developer, plotting out a housing development and giving streets the sort of names our 1800 John Brown gave to the townships in his tract. Imagine, if you can, living at 42 Regularity Boulevard! Or 391 Chastity Lane. Or on Sobriety Drive! No, it wouldn't do at all today. We need . . . we are accustomed to different sorts of names. So we have the other side of the coin of the "One Man's Meat Law:" the fashions of the ges vary, and what seems strange to one generation may be perfectly normal to another.

Where then are we in respect to names in the Adirondacks? Why, where common sense puts us! We're looking now for names that almost all of us—if not every one of us—would see as "different." Not because we live in a different time or age, but because they are . . . "different!" And why in the world would we want to bother looking at such names? Well, I guess because they're there, and even more, because they're fun. We'll relish the pleasure of a good chuckle at a funny name, and we'll shake our heads in admiration of the inventiveness, the imagination, the elan of those who "came up" with that name.

We'll just have some fun with some Adirondack names.

Who knows what they'll give us besides a smile and a laugh.

Have you ever been to the hamlet of "North Granville Truthville" in Washington County? Quite honestly, I haven't. But its name beckons me, and it is on my list of important places to visit! Although a bit outside the Adirondacks proper, I couldn't resist mentioning it. Actually all of what is now Clinton, Essex, Warren, Franklin and Saratoga Counties were once part of Washington County, so in a way it is Adirondackian. Anyway, the name is so . . . so . . . so *true* to itself that it deserves greater fame. There are also in Washington County the communities of "Granville" itself, "South Granville," and "West Granville Corners." "East Granville" appears not to have made it. But it is "North Granville Truthville" that captures my imagination and admiration.

Oneida County gives us a community known only as "Parts." Perhaps that's what stimulated "Eureka!" Some St. Lawrence County residents live in "Slab City;" others in "Kokomo Corners." A list of communities which includes the likes of "Kokomo Corners," "Slab City," "Eureka," "Parts," and "North Granville Truthville" is worthy of the charge of being less than responsible in terms of the importance of having a "good" name. These names evoke a flavor of the impertinent, a hint at the thumbing of one's nose at propriety. And that helps bring the smile to our lips.

But by and large, the forces of serious and respectable society dominated our village naming. Creating and settling a community was—and still is—serious business, and the name of your home is even more serious business. So most communities boast names that are SERIOUS AND RESPECTABLE. Not only that, but the larger units, the counties, all boast IMPORTANT and FAMOUS names. Washington, Jefferson, Franklin and Hamilton Counties are all very FAMOUS and IMPORTANT. Clinton and Lewis Counties are early GOVERNORS. Fulton County of STEAMBOAT fame. And as the King of Siam says, "Etcetera, Etcetera."

County and community names, then, generally can be counted on to reflect a sober and serious view. And we've seen that for the most part our elevations seem too grand to allow for much levity. Nevertheless, as we are constantly reminded, human playfulness will out, and so we do find a few odd and humorous mountain names.

Fulton County boasts a "Lawyer Mountain," perhaps in traditional Adirondack disdain for the legal profession (a 19th century visitor to Saranac Lake described it as a community blessed, for it harbored no lawyer within its borders). Hamilton County contributes "Mount Overrocker," a case of elevated onomatopoeia, I believe. Saratoga County offers us the delicious "Day Center Mountain." One sees visions of pre-schoolers climbing great heights. "Sporting Hill" comes from Franklin County. And Essex County gives us the miracle of "Gizzle Ocean Mountain" (without the 'r' in 'gizzle').

Although most Adirondack heights do wear elevated names, the likes of "Sporting Hill," "Mount Overrocker," "Lawyer Mountain," "Day Center Mountain," and "Gizzle Ocean Mountain" remind us of the fun it is to be human and eccentric.

Since remote brooks and ponds often escaped the gaze of the serious and important folk who tend to stay on the beaten path, and since the explorers and early settlers of these out of the way places often saw the world in "earthier" colors, and since pretension and formality hold court most often in places far removed from the backwaters, given all these "sinces," we might expect to find some water names that are eccentric and amusing.

I've always enjoyed the notion of "Sly Pond." And there are two of them, one in Washington County and the other in Hamilton County. It is possible that it came from the Dutch "vly," so common in the Adirondacks, but SLY is so much more fun.

Hamilton County is also blessed with oddly contradictory water names: "Dry Lake," "Unknown Pond," "O K Slip Brook," and "O K Slip Pond." If it's OK to slip, perhaps the lake better be dry! But where in the world is "Unknown Pond"? Hamilton County gives us a few other eyebrow raisers: "Antediluvian Pond," "Bum Pond," and "Helldiver Pond." I'll spare you the bad puns.

Herkimer County chips in with the enigmatic "Why Pond." Warren County's "Rodunk Brook" reminds us of America's wonderful "Podunk." And Franklin County serves up the lovely "Pork Barrel Pond" as well as "Humbug Brook," and, as if commenting upon itself, "Slang Pond." We go back to Essex County for its "Overshot Pond," "Hot Water Pond," "Bullpout Pond" (there's a "Bullhead Pond" too, but that's pretty ordinary, but 'bullpout' . . . that's something else), and finally that companion to that miracle of a mountain name, Essex County gives us "Grizzle Ocean." And it is spelled with the 'r' this time.

And so, amongst others in this land of beautiful waters, we have these eccentric names throughout the Adirondacks: "Sly," "Dry," "Unknown," "O K Slip," "Antediluvian," "Bum," "Helldiver," "Rodunk," "Pork Barrel," "Humbug," "Slang," "Overshot," "Hot Water," "Bullpout," "Grizzle Ocean," and "Why."

Roads in the backwoods, perhaps even more so than in urban areas, are the lifeline to survival. People know their roads; they deal with them in winter storms and spring muds. And, as with mountains and lakes and settlements, when we get off the beaten track we discover the human quality of individual, earthy, non-pretentious, humorously felt notions of the world. No Interstate 101 for the likes of us. Our roads tell us things!

Sometimes they tell us where we're going, like Clinton County's "Gougeville Spring Road," even when there's no "Gougeville Spring" to go to! Sometimes roads tell us about themselves, and when they do we often get a chuckle out of it. Can you imagine the prospect of a Sunday drive in St. Lawrence County along "Toothaker Road?" It's enough to get you on to "Stammer Road" in the same county.

There are lots of "Plank Roads" throughout the Adirondacks, a memory of the days when roads were built by laying planks of wood along a pathway. And Essex County still boasts a "Corduroy Road" as well; imagine putting logs down across a dirt pathway, like the ridges on an old-fashioned washboard, and bumping your way over that! That's a long way from Herkimer County's "Top Notch Road."

Lewis County 'fesses up to a "Muck Road," as well as a "Rock Road" and "Stone Road." Not very attractive. My favorite from Lewis County is "Hell's Kitchen Road." Talk about taking the City into the Country! Oneida County also has a "Muck Road" and goes far enough to warn us about its "Hazard

Road." It editorializes its own "Golly Road" and boasts of "Big Ed's Road." Washington County brags about a "Best Road," and Saratoga County not only has a "Radar Road," but also an "Atomic Project Road" along with an earlier "Bump Road."

The list of roadways, of ways of getting from one place to another is long and rich. From St. Lawrence County: "Chevrolet," "Cream of the Valley," "Crobar," "Crusher," "Dandy," "Dollar," "Poor," "Vice," "Brooklyn," "Kansas," "Bagdad," "Bull Run," and "Sitting Bull." From Warren County: "4-H" and "Short" as well as "Back to Sodom;" from Herkimer County: "Hooper Dooper" and "Tea Cup;" from Clinton County: "Devil's Den." These roads and streets deserve to be framed and admired, and the finest compliment to them is our admiring silence. After all, why spoil a good joke by explaining it?

Freedom is wonderful. It gives us the space to be and to become. It gives us the opportunity to explore the universe and articulate it for ourselves, to break through the formulas of thought and speech and describe experience in our own unique way. It is that breakthrough that makes our eccentric names so human and enjoyable, so unexpected and durable.

But freedom also gives us the space to be destructive when we violate the norms and expectations and formulae of our culture. Sometimes when we violate the norms of our culture, we violate the integrity of other people. And often this occurs when we use names that diminish us all. It is the sense of the destructiveness, of the violation of human integrity, that forces this editorial intrusion into our story of Adirondack names.

There are two types of names that are unsuitable for every one in every age. These names demean ethnic groups and insult the human body. They are neither amusing nor clever nor enriching; what they are, is brutal, destructive, and dehumanizing. Other than as reminders of the worst in us, these names have no place on our geographic or psychic landscapes.

One may defend a "Frenchtown" or an "Irish Settlement Road," pointing out that there is nothing demeaning about identifying the national or ethnic characteristics of a settlement or feature. This seems reasonably common sensical. After all, there's nothing wrong with calling a Frenchman a Frenchman or an Irishwoman an Irishwoman. Some may even defend an

"Indian Point." "Indians," I'm sure, would disagree, calling for their preferred "Native American," or even less political "Amerindian." See how easy it is to move into a linguistic no-man's land when we talk about "Indian Point." See how easy it may be to demean people, even when we don't mean to?

See how easy it is to slip from an "Indian Point" to a "Polack Pond" in the Adirondacks. It happens when we don't watch our step, when we become psychically careless and don't feel the destructive power in the name. It is when the identification represents a vile prejudice conjuring up a history of brutal exploitation that we have slipped . . . no, fallen into a shameful place. Names which identify national or ethnic character are not, in themselves, demeaning. But names which represent the stereotypical targeting of people for ridicule, injustice and abuse demean all of us. If we haven't become sensitive enough to object to "Indian Point," we *should* be ready to object to "Polack Pond," and there *must* be shame in anybody willing to abide by "Niggerhead Mountain." The glories of Adirondack names are not without their sadder moments.

In a great many other parts of the country, names suggestive of or reflective of puerile interests and sexual exploitation have been deleted with Victorian zeal. "Ass Ridges" have been expunged; "Buttocks Hills" have been bowdlerized; "Maidenheads" vanish; "Cuckold Town" (Staten Island, New York) rejected; even "Bull Rock" was too sexual and became "Man Cow Rock!" Sometimes the line between a realistic and vibrant sexuality and prudish temerity is difficult for some to draw. Sometimes the censorship seems silly. But we still retain "Bitch" as well as "Nippletop" Mountain. These names reflect sexist, if not puerile, responses. And again, the only value in recording them is to remind us of how far we've still got to go, baby.

11

Where Do We Go From Here?

A few years ago a friend at the United States Board of Geographic Names, which, by the way, has taken on the overwhelming task of attempting to locate and map every place in the country, told me about a telephone conversation he'd had with someone from Illinois. It seemed that this gentleman lived in a pleasant and convivial "retirement community" which boasted, along with a social hall, planned entertainment, golf course and well maintained walks and landscaping, a little, natural body of water called "Lake Serenity."

My friend and I were quick to pick up on "Lake Serenity." More than likely, we agreed, "Lake Serenity" emerged as an advertising alternative by the local land developer who felt that "Quicksand Outlet" or "Skunk Hollow" or some other prior local name would not help sales. Be that as it may, this apparently very active retirement community enjoyed "Lake Serenity," according to the gentleman from Illinois, who claimed to be an unofficial spokesperson for the citizens of this settlement. He said that he and his wife regularly enjoyed the rowing on "Lake Serenity," and they, along with a great many other citizens of the community, felt that the waterway was an important part of the pleasure of their lives.

Recently, he went on, a group had made an excursion to a shopping mall, expressly to see a movie with Katherine Hepburn and Henry Fonda. The movie was so touching, so pertinent to their lives, that they wanted to rename their little pond. Surely it would be a relatively simple task, one that would give an added pleasure to an entire community, to rename their water retreat "Golden Pond!"

Unfortunately for these good people in Illinois, but in some ways fortunately for the rest of us, "Golden Pond" remains the name of this movie, not this waterway. My friend speculates that there must have been close to two hundred and fifty calls requesting that "Golden Pond" replace a name currently affixed to lakes and ponds throughout movie-going America. So much for the power of Hollywood!

Not easily can names be changed to suit fads or whims. There is the already noted United States Board of Geographic Names, which oversees place-name recording throughout the United States, and each of the fifty states maintains an office or official or a coordinating board of citizens—unsalaried—to consider recommendations and suggestions for name changes. This screening process does ensure that we don't become flooded with "Golden Ponds;" on the other hand, these layers of "official" determiners do inhibit the creation of new or newer names.

The naming of our new world moved from an initial openness of possibility and the use of the new, in landscape and language, to the formal and structured "official" concerns of social and political pressures. In this, name-giving lays claim to a place beside other creative acts.

The earliest explorers and settlers took what was at hand, molded it with the habits and traditions brought with them, and, with an almost universal openness and unselfconsciousness, gave names to the unnamed. They evoked their own sensibilities to describe the landscape, to memorialize their previous homes, to honor their great. The more "official" the character of the adventures, the more "official" the names bestowed by them; conversely, the less "official," the less hampered they were by social and governmental pressures, the more the personal and descriptive names tended toward the common and familiar, the earthy and scatological.

When we see names like "Joe Pond," "Lake Champlain," "Buck Pond," "Mount Pisgah," "Devils Wash Dish," "Schroon River," "Bald Peak," "Lake George," "Raquette," "Plattsburgh,"

"Essex," "Keeseville," "Bitch Mountain," "Grassy Pond," "Mud Pond," "Ticonderoga," "Sugarbush" and "Nippletop Mountain," we feel we are back among our early explorers and settlers. These names describe, commemorate, evoke God or His enemy, conjure up a previous home, call attention to the human body. In short, these names reflect the sort of sensibility we often—in our own romantic frailty—like to think of as lusty Elizabethan.

After this first stage had ripened and the early maps had set the names in ink (if not in concrete), other pressures began to be felt, all under the caveat of the spreading civilization. In our neck of the woods, these pressures took two forms: the Neo-classic and the Romantic. And as in almost all other creative thrusts, they may appear as opposites but we know they are from the same stamp, sides of the same coin.

The neo-classic imprint on our landscape goes beyond the Greek pillars of southern plantation homes and state capital buildings made popular under the influence of that great democrat, Thomas Jefferson, and others. The revival of Greek and Roman ideals in this "new world" is to be seen not only in the architecture of 1795 to 1840; it can also be read on our touring guides and road maps.

You can cross the length of New York State, for example, following the Erie Canal, which was followed by the New York Central Railroad, and now by the Thomas E. Dewey Thruway, from Albany to Buffalo, and revisit the classic period of Hellenic and Roman times! "Troy," "Syracuse," "Ithaca," "Ilion," "Manlius," "Cicero," "Homer" are "just a few," as they say in novice writing classes, of the settlements named during this neo-classic period. We'd like to include the Roman, Seneca, at the western end of the Greek continuum, but our "Seneca" comes from the Native American, not the Roman. Here in the Adirondacks, despite its rural tradition, we celebrate the classics with our "Minerva," "Diana," "Corinth" and "Massena."

It is in the use of some Native American names that we see one part of the other side of the name-coin, the Romantic. Carl Sandburg, following Walt Whitman, among others (another quick fix for novice writers), sings of the mellifluous and mysterious sounds of the names as they roll off the tongue. "Monongahela," "Allegheny," "Susquehanna," "Ohio,"

"Shenandoah," "Mississippi," "Tonawanda" are names that echo across the land.

Here in the Adirondacks we make our romantic music with the likes of "Ticonderoga," "Saratoga," "Akwesasne," "Onchiota," "Tahawus," "Toowarloondah" (Blue Mountain Lake) and, of course, "Adirondack."

The other part of this romantic side of the name coin gives our landscape an international flavor unique in the world. We have been a melting pot of peoples, to be sure, and we are also a kaleidoscope of places. We have been charged, at times, with being parochial, but in our names we are the most cosmopolitan of nations! When you look at the American landscape, you can see the entire world, from Aberdeen to Zurich and all the stops between.

Here in the Adirondacks we enjoy the exotic hints of "Bombay," "Madrid," "Santa Clara," "Hague," "Galway," "Bangor," "Stockholm," "Brighton," "Lisbon," "Cork," "Antwerp" and "Northampton" as well as "Norway," "Poland" and "Russia." Some, surely, are transfer names, but just as surely some offer a taste of the exotic and alien, a hint at the possibilities of adventure and mystery. If the first, earlier stage can be called Elizabethan with its feel of LUSTY REALITY COUPLED WITH PASSIONATE RELIGIOSITY, this second, neo-classic/romantic period may be described as STATELY POWER SPICED WITH IMAGINATIVE SENSIBILITY. We have moved from the glories of Shakespeare to the dark brilliances of Wordsworth, Keats, and Coleridge.

We entered a third stage of name-giving in the Adirondacks in the mid-nineteenth century (more or less), and are still in it. We moved from the Neo-classic and Romantic to the Victorian: the world of cultured and practical sensibilities, the world of decorum placed in the service of pragmatic commercialism. The names from this movement insinuate themselves onto our landscape next to our Elizabethan, Neo-classic and Romantic visions.

We are confronted with the likes of "Laphams Mills" near our Peru; "Port Kent" overlooks Lake Champlain; there is a "Moffitsville"—on the Saranac. "Whippleville" is a suburb of Malone; there is a "Doctors Lake" near Wawbeek. "Olmsted-ville" neighbors Minerva and Irishtown.

As the Adirondacks attracted settlers to its mines and forests and farms, villages and hamlets sprang up throughout the North Country. Communities were established and called themselves "Starbuckville," "Huletts Station," "Conifer," "Benson Mines," "Moshier Falls," "Thurman," "Batcheller-ville," "Pottersville," "Wells," "Knappville," "Coffins Mills," "Newton Falls," "Aldrich," "Peters Corners," "Clarksboro," and on and on and on. These names measure the growth of the Adirondacks from the 1840s to the 1890s and reflect the soberly serious nature of the task of getting on in life and building civilization in this northern wilderness.

"Eagle Eyrie" looks down upon Rattlesnake Knob, when we get on in life and build civilization in the Adirondacks; just so the newer names of housing developments, for example, multiply and prosper: "Beechwood" and "Glendale" and "Fawn Ridge" and "Riverview Heights" and "Birch Knoll." These "appealing" names supersede older neighborhoods like French Hill, Irishtown and Timbuktu.

Although it appears at a casual glance that this present period is uninspired and dull when it comes to making and giving names, this verdict may be unwarranted. Granted, there is a great deal of social pressure exerted to ensure conventional and "proper" names. Granted, there is a structured and official governmental presence. Granted, then, that public and private forms of censorship inhibit a free play of name possibilities: a "GP" rating seems necessary for official survival (and considering the names representing sexual and ethnic slurs, this censorship does have some validity). Granted all this, there is cause for optimism.

The same drives to name places in the Adirondacks as we have done before work in us now. We still describe new places; we continue to commemorate events and heroes; we insist upon molding the landscape with the stamp of our own names; we eternally call upon the Bible as well as the classics; we always refer to our past homes and transfer them to our new frontiers; we continually embrace new peoples and place non-American names upon the American anvil; and we inexorably insist upon the freedom of the spirit to defy all the rules and pressures as we nourish the excitement and vitality underlying all our innovative and "funny" and "odd" names.

My optimism was reinforced when I came across an article in a local Adirondack newspaper. Although the reporter's story was about some personal and "nicknames" of people in Lake Placid, the response to the article and these "nicknames" holds truths for us about the names of places.

The reporter begins with a statement we can certainly relate to in terms of place names, even though the headline was "Exploring the Origins of Unique Local Nicknames." He writes, "Oldtimers here recall their childhood days with clarity, but the origins of their own nicknames are often shrouded in mystery." When asked how he came by the nickname *Beaner,* an informant was quoted as saying, "I can't tell you. My father had it and he passed it on." The article lists these reported nicknames in addition to *Beaner: Toot, Peanut, Jumbo, Rip, Baldy* and *Moon.*

These nicknames appeared in the *Lake Placid News,* Wednesday, October 14, 1987. The list is certainly informal and amusing, and the commentary about how these nicknames emerged supplies another layer of folklore interest.

Three weeks passed before a letter to the editor appeared in the November 4 issue. The author, a fellow who had grown up in Lake Placid, states, and I am sure the reporter would agree, that the article "is just the tip of the iceberg." He then offers a list from the days of his youth, noting that he'd "be interested in seeing more. There are many I've failed to recall." This list of nicknames includes: *Hairdo, Sly, Pudge, Moose, Omaley, Gooey, Pugsly, Toad, Wiz, Rabbit, Snake, Fatbelly, Blue Flats, Twenty, Presto, Weasel, Peaches, Naj, XL, Too Far, Pockets, Famous, Beaver, Chi-Chi, Resin* and *Mild Bill.*

The original article focused on how the nicknames emerged and less on the nicknames themselves, whereas the author of the letter to the editor was interested in giving us his list of remembered names. So it is understandable that the second list included many more nicknames than did the reporter's story. Therefore, let's look not so much at the number of nicknames as at the character of these names. Contrast the seven listed in the original article (*Beaner, Toot, Peanut, Jumbo, Rip, Baldy* and *Moon*) with seven taken from the letter to the editor: *Hairdo, Fatbelly, Toad, Gooey, Pudge, Resin* and *Blue Flats* (putting aside all the rest of the *Prestos* and *Weasels* and *Omaleys*).

There is a qualitative difference. The nicknames hunted up by the reporter seem mildly interesting and occasionally amusing as well as informal and less than "proper." They are, indeed, names that go beyond what one expects people to be known by in the serious nature of the task of getting on in life.

But the names offered us in the letter to the editor! These are names by which young people in Lake Placid of only a few years ago knew each other. Look again at these nicknames: *Gooey, Fatbelly, Resin* and all the rest. Not only are they occasionally amusing and informal and not too "proper" and unexpected, they also smack of earthiness, of creativity, of a vitality that breaks the rules, of youthful exuberance. Read these names and remember your own youth and your own disdain for the respectable and the proper and the need to get on with the serious business of getting on.

I offer the suggestion that if we can scratch the skin of officialdom and formality, if we can become familiar enough with the people who have lived in the Adirondacks all their lives and whose roots go back to the earlier days, if we can tap the sources of folk memory and usage, we'll find names for places in the Adirondacks as unexpected, as improper, as creative, as funny, as joyfully celebratory of life as the best of our nicknames.

So it may be that I've been a bit too hard on "American Victorian" and our present age. After all, Dickens did leave us Tom Thumb and Scrooge! It may be merely that every age sees the past as a time more open to innovation and creativity in the way names are made. Perhaps that's because we don't experience the limits and restrictions they felt; we only experience our own. Perhaps the twenty-first century will look back at the names we make in the twentieth century and delight in our creativity.

However it does seem that we'll never know a time again when it was possible to put on maps the kinds of names that were given to the landscape of our Adirondacks. So we must commemorate those names as a way of helping to understand our past, just as we delight in those names because they make us laugh. Come with me then, on a fantasy tour through time and landscape. Fasten your seatbelts but throw away your tour maps. They won't help you on this trip.

In Essex County alone, we can visit *North Pole* if we follow *Klondike Brook,* which starts near *Lake Tear-of-the-Clouds.* If that's too intemperate, one can enjoy *Warm Pond* or even *Hot Water Pond,* a few miles from *The Devil's Wash Dish,* above which is *Fairy Ladder Falls,* which spills into *Breakneck Brook.* Essex County is a most encompassing place, boasting its own *Rome, Timbuktu* and *Texas Ridge,* from which one can see *Napoleon's Cap. Honey Pond* is on the way to *Pudding Hollow,* separated from *Pepper Hollow* by *Pack Horse Mountain.* To the East are the *Pyramid Lakes* and *Pharaoh Mountains,* the *Hills of Hebron* and *Mt. Pisgah.* Farther west are *Quaker Mountain* and *Pulpit Rock.* Those of another inclination can always follow *OK Slip Falls* to *Tight Nipping,* which leads to *Jug Pond* and the two *Jug Mountains.* If you keep *Bum Pond* on your right and find the six *Lost Ponds,* you'll climb *Poke-O-Moonshine* and look down on *Grog Harbor.* By this time you'll enjoy *The Devil's Punch Bowl,* which is adjacent to *Devil's Pulpit* and *Devil's Oven. Babble Pond* leads to *Dunk Pond,* which seems in order at this stage; then on to *Coffee Pond,* which is near *Sober Kiln* on the way to *Saints Rest. Shanty Bottom Brook* starts in the village of *Mossy,* and from the village of *Look* one can see *Loch Bonnie,* and the area of five *Clear Ponds.* There are, however, near *Gizzle (no "r") Ocean Mountain* and *Grizzle (with an "r") Ocean Pond,* a full dozen *Mud Ponds;* they lie, of course, close to *Bitch Mountain.*

Ah, the zest for life, the lustiness, the romantic and quixotic, the rejection of pomp, the pleasure in the profane and the humorous! Still, there is hope for our time. We are inordinately fond of creation and invention and change. And no more so than with words and names. Nothing is "set in concrete." Everything is open and possible. Witness this grand old story: An English couple doing the Grand Tour of our Americas made their pilgrimage to a shrine famous throughout Europe. They came to Niagara Falls to gaze with awe upon this manifestation of America's grandness. They returned home to talk of their American trip, with special reference to Niagara Falls. But in a land where the natives had evolved into pronouncing "Worcestershire" as *wustisha,* and "Herefordshire" as *hefidsha,* and "Salisbury" as *sawlzbri,* our English couple was cautioned in no uncertain terms that they must learn that they had visited not "Niagara Falls" but *Niffles!*

Not only may we recreate with the youthful informality of "nicknames" and with the transferred habits of pronunciation; we may also create by discovery.

After Mt. Pisgah's wintry scene had softened, leaving us to the glories of Adirondack summer, we took the opportunity of exploring a bend in the river with Canadian friends, Andre and Huguette Lapierre. Both Andre and Huguette are linguists and lovers of names as well as teachers and translators. A bit of a rain shower led us to beach our boat and settle in the protection of a sheltered grove. We watched a heron looking for its lunch. We listened to the mild rain and the music of life in the branches over us. We looked at the bank of the river water and the heron and the water lily pads. We ourselves lunched, perhaps in sympathetic encouragement to the heron, and we talked of . . . nothing especially important. A romantically idyllic scene.

When we left our hideaway, we took with us a moment that will return again and again. It is here now as I write about it. And that landscape in ourselves is duplicated on the bend in the river. It was a discovery both external and in ourselves. I can show you *Rainbow Bower* whenever you wish.

Index

For the reader's convenience, a General Index precedes the Geographic (Place) Name Index. "The" is used only when it is an integral part of the name, such as "The Pines." Designations such as "County," "Township," "Lake," "River," are used only when essential for clarity. Native American names have been crossreferenced with English names when appropriate. The General Index lists the nicknames discussed in Chapter 11. Finally, names referring to the Adirondacks, such as "North Country," "North Woods," and "Adirondack Mountains," occur on almost every page of the book and are therefore listed in the index only when the discussion concerns the origin of the name or refers to the word solely as a name. For example the word "Adirondacks" in the sentence, ". . . in this part of the Adirondacks, . . ." is not listed.

General Index

Abolitionist, 14, 20, 37, 69
Aboriginal Place Names of New York, 66, 102
Adirondack Daily Enterprise, 65
Adirondack Forest Preserve, 94, 124
Adirondack Iron Works, 74
Adirondack Mountain Club, 95
Adirondack Murray, 65, 85
Adirondack Park, 13, 99, 124, 125
American Tragedy, An, 15
Arnold, Benedict, 56
Astor, John Jacob, 69

Baker, Milote, 66
Baldy, 146
Barkeaters, The, 24
Bartleby The Scrivener, 52
Bartok, Bela, 14
Beaner, 146
Beauchamp, William, 66, 102, 104

Beaver, 146
Bernstein, Leonard, 14
Bert LaFountain's Packard, 84
Bethune, Norman, 14
Blagden, Thomas, 65
Blood, Orlando, 66
Blue Flats, 146
Blue Line, The, 123, 124, 125, 126
Bonaparte, Joseph, 15, 86, 109
Bonaparte, Napoleon, 15, 109
Boston Tea Party, 20, 62
Brant, Joseph, 41
Brant, Molly, 41, 42
Brown, John (of North Elba), 14, 20, 25, 37, 61, 68, 69, 70
Brown, John (of Rhode Island), 14, 20, 22, 25, 37, 38, 61, 62, 63, 134
Bumppo, Natty, 14, 40, 41
Burr, Aaron, 14, 62

Cabot, John, 15
Cantor, Eddie, 14
Capone, Al, 68, 70
Carson, Russell, 95
Cartier, Jacques, 15, 93
Castorland, 53, 109
Cayuga, 71
Champlain, Samuel, 92, 93
Charlotte, Princess, 31
Chaucer, Geoffrey, 116
Chazy, Sieur, 72
Cheney, John, 75
Chi-Chi, 146
Chingachgook, 40, 41
Civil War, 14, 61, 69, 76, 109, 114
Columbus, Christopher, 15
Colvin, Verplanck, 65
Compagnie de New York, 53, 68
Constable, William, 52, 53, 54, 68
Cooper, James Fenimore, 14, 40, 41
Corey, Jesse, 65
Cortlands (Family), 54
Curler, Arendt Van, 16
Cyrano de Bergerac, 108

Debtor's Prison, 53, 58
Deerslayer, 14, 85
Deerslayer, The, 40
*Descriptive Guide to the
    Adirondacks,* 86
Dexter, Orlando, 115
Diamond, "Legs", 14
Dickens, Charles, 53, 147
Digs (see Fourth Name Law),
    45, 46
Domestic (see Third Name Law),
    45, 46
Donaldson, Alfred L., 66
Dreiser, Theodore, 15
Dunning, Alvah, 65
Durant, William, 65
Dutch West India Company, 16

Einstein, Albert, 14, 20
Emerson, Ralph Waldo, 14
Emmons, Ebenezer, 22, 24, 58, 59
Erie Canal, 61, 143

Fadden, John, 90
Fadden, Ray, 90

Famous, 146
Fatbelly, 146, 147
Flower, Governor Roswell, 59
Fonda, Henry, 141
Foster, Nat, 40, 85
French and Indian War, 18, 50, 56,
    83, 93
Frost, Robert, 26
Fulton, Robert, 59, 61

George III, King of England, 31, 42
Gilliland, Bess, 54, 55
Gilliland, Charlotte, 54, 55
Gilliland, Elizabeth, 54, 55
Gilliland, James, 54, 55, 56
Gilliland, William, 30, 54, 55, 56, 57,
    58, 74, 97
Golden Pond, 45
Gooey, 146, 147

Hairdo, 146
Hamilton, Alexander, 14, 53
Harison, Richard, 49, 50
Headley, Joel Tyler, 65
Henderson, David, 73, 74, 75, 89
Henry IV, King of France, 50
Hepburn, Katherine, 141
Herreshoff, Frederick, 37, 38, 61, 62
*Historical Sketches of Northern
    New York and the Adirondack
    Wilderness,* 22
Hudson Bay Company, 69
Hudson, Henry, 92, 93
Hurd, John, 76, 77
Huron, 24

Iroquois Confederacy, 89

Jefferson, Thomas, 143
*John Brown's Tract: Lost
    Adirondack Empire,* 61
Johnson, Sir John, 41, 42, 43, 100
Johnson, Sir William, 41, 42, 93,
    108
Jolson, Al, 14
Jumbo, 146

Keese, William, 109

L'Hommedieu, Ezra, 49

LaFountain, Bert, 83, 84
Lake Placid News, 146
Lapierre, Andre and Huguette, 149
LeMoyne, Simon, 18
LeRay, James, 109
Livingston, Philip, 62
Livingstons (Family), 50, 55
Lone Ranger, 40
Louis XIII, King of France,
    107, 108

Macomb, Alexander, 50, 52, 53
Macomb, Major General Alexander,
    20
Macomb Purchase, 23, 49, 50, 51, 52,
    53, 54, 63, 67
Macomb Syndicate, 49
Macy, Rowland H., 65
Malone, Edmond, 49
Manahatins, 100
Marcy, Governor William L., 58
Marcy's Mantle (see Fifth Name
    Law), 59
Martin, Steve, 65
McAlpin, William, 65
McCormick, Daniel, 52, 53, 54
McIntyre, Archibald, 74, 75
McKinley, William, 14
Melville, Herman, 52
Mencken, H. L., 132
Mild Bill, 146
Miller, Pliny, 66
Montauks, 100
Moody, Jacob Smith, 66
Moody, Mart, 65
Moon, 146
Moose, 146
Morgan, J. Pierpont, 14
Morgenthau, Henry, 65
Morton, Levi, 65
Mostly Spruce and Hemlock, 75

Naj, 146
Names:
    Biblical, 31, 32, 33, 35, 60, 64
    Classical, 31, 32, 33, 35
    Commemorative, 31, 33, 35, 59, 60,
        64, 91, 93, 94, 96, 100, 102, 106,
        107, 113, 114, 115
    Descriptive, 32, 33, 35, 88, 94, 95,

96, 102, 103, 107, 114, 142
Dutch, 26, 29, 92, 110, 111, 113, 114,
    117, 136
Eccentric, 27, 28, 32, 33, 35, 60, 64,
    113, 114, 136
Episodic, 91, 102, 103, 104, 114
Fanciful, see Eccentric Names
Foreign, 30, 33, 35
French, 26, 29, 41, 43, 44, 55, 66, 71,
    80, 93, 94, 96, 106, 107, 110, 113,
    114, 117, 131
German, 113, 117
Laws:
    Fifth, 59, 60
    First, 43, 45
    Fourth, 45, 46
    Second, 44, 45
    Seventh, 133
    Sixth, 119, 120, 122
    Native American, 26, 28, 29, 40, 41,
        43, 66, 67, 80, 85, 90, 91, 94, 96,
        101, 102, 103, 105, 106, 107, 110,
        113, 114, 117, 143
    Personal, 30, 33, 35, 59, 60, 64, 88,
        91, 94, 95, 96, 100, 102, 114, 119,
        142
    Scottish, 29, 110, 113, 117
    Transfer, 31, 33, 35, 60, 64, 114,
        122
    Water, 88, 89, 91, 94, 136
Names on the Land, 120
New York Central Railroad, 53, 77,
    109, 143
Nicknames, 146, 147
Nicolaisen, Wilhelm, 43
No Ditto (see Sixth Name Law),
    119, 122
Normans, 116
Nye, Bill, 96

Olympic Region, 113
Omaley, 146
One Man's Meat (see Seventh Name
Law), 133, 134
Oneida, 71
Onondaga, 71
Ozymandias, 30

Peaches, 146
Peaks and People of the Adirondacks, 95

Peanut, 146
Pearl Harbored, 44
People of the Long House, 16
Phelps, Old Mountain, 85, 96
Platt, Zephaniah, 29, 71
Plumley, Honest John, 65, 85
Pockets, 146
Post, Marjorie, 86, 115
Presto, 146
Prohibition, 70, 84, 104
Promised Land, The, 47, 63
Pudge, 146
Pugsley, 146
Puritan Virtues, 37, 63

Rabbit, 146
Racket, The (see First Law of Names), 43, 46
Read, Allen Walker, 107, 132
Rensselaers (Family), 55
Resin, 146, 147
Revolutionary War, 14, 20, 31, 37, 40, 41, 50, 52, 56, 62
Rip, 146
Rock Clan, 24
Rockefeller, William G., 14, 65, 86, 115
Rogers, Major Robert, 83, 85
Rogers Rangers, 83
Rogers, Will, 14
Rondeau, Noah John, 85
Roosevelt, Teddy, 14, 65

Sabael, 74, 100
Sabattis, Captain Peter, 42, 43, 100
Sabattis, Mitchell, 65
Sandberg, Carl, 143
Schultz, "Dutch", 14
Schuylers (Family), 55
Seneca, 71
Shangri-La, 44
Six Nation Indian Museum, 90
Skaroon, Madame, 108
Sly, 146
Smith, Gerrit, 69
Smith, Paul, 65, 84
Smith, Peter, 68, 69
Snake, 146
Stevenson, Robert L., 14

Stewart, George R., 120
Stickney, Benjamin, 114, 115
Stillman, W. J., 65
Stink Hole (see Second Name Law), 44, 46
Stoddard, S. R., 65
Street, Alfred Billings, 65
Stuyvesant, Peter, 16, 107
Sylvester, Nathaniel B., 22, 87

Tait, Arthur F., 65
Tale of Two Cities, A, 53
Thoreau, Henry David, 36
Through-Much-Trial-and-Tribulation-We-Enter-The-Kingdom-of-Heaven Lindloff, 27
Tiffany, Louis C., 65
Toad, 146
Tonto, 40
Too Far, 146
Toot, 146
Trudeau, Dr. Edward L., 65, 66
Twain, Mark, 14, 40, 41
Twenty, 146

United States Board of Geographic Names, 114, 141, 142

Van Dyke, Henry, 65
Van Schuyler, 29
Vanderbilt, Cornelius, 14, 76, 77, 86, 89, 115

Wall Street, 52, 54
Wallace, Edwin, 86
War of 1812, 14, 20
Washington, George, 14, 52
Waterloo, 44
Weasel, 146
Webb, William Seward, 76, 77, 89, 105, 115
Wheeler, William, 65
Whitman, Walt, 25, 143
Whitney, William C., 86
Winchester, Caleb T., 65
Wiz, 146

XL, 146

Geographic (Place) Name Index

Aberdeen, 144
Abe's Hill, 96
Aderondackx (see Adirondacks), 24
Adirondack, 37, 67, 144
Adirondack Group, The, 24
Adirondack Mountains, The, 25
Adirondacks, The, 24, 25, 26
Akwesasne, 28, 101, 144
Albany, 13, 20, 29, 39, 41, 42, 52, 55, 56, 68, 72, 74, 77, 88, 92, 103, 110, 111, 143
Aldrich, 145
Algonquin Peak, 96, 100
Allegheny, 143
Allen Mountain, 95
Antediluvian Pond, 136, 137
Antwerp, 144
Archer Vly, 112
Arendahronon (see Adirondacks), 24
Armstrong Mountain, 95
Arundaks (see Adirondacks), 24
Ass Ridge, 139
Atomic Project Road, 138
Attiwandaronk (see Adirondacks), 24
Ausable Forks, 44, 65
Ausable River, 24, 29, 71, 88, 107, 114, 131
Avacal, 15, 16, 17, 20, 25, 37, 108

Babble Pond, 148
Back Road, 33
Back to Sodom Road, 138
Bagdad Road, 138
Baker's, 66
Bald Hill, 97
Bald Mountain, 97, 115, 116
Bald Peak, 142
Balm of Gilead Mountain, 32, 63
Bangor, 60, 144
Basin Mountain, 95
Batchellerville, 145
Batten Kill, 111
Beantown, 13
Bear Mountain, 32
Bear Pond, 126
Beaver Brook, 32
Beaver Flow, 89
Beaver Pond, 126, 131
Beechwood, 145

Bennet's Pond, 70, 71
Benson Mines, 145
Bessboro, 55, 58
Best Road, 138
Beverwyk, 111
Big Apple, The, 13, 29, 70, 100, 107
Big Ed's Road, 138
Big Pond, 89
Big Slide Mountain, 95, 96
Billy Mountain, 97
Birch Knoll, 145
Birmingham, 110
Bitch Mountain, 139, 143, 148
Black River, 13
Blake's Peak, 95
Bloodville, 27, 66
Bloody Pond, 31, 73, 89
Blue Mountain Lake, 41, 64, 144
Bolton's Landing, 30
Bombay, 144
Boston, 13, 20
Botheration Pond, 33, 126
Bouquet River, 55
Breakneck Brook, 148
Brighton, 144
Broadway, 29, 110
Bronx, The, 29, 53, 110
Brooklyn, 29
Brooklyn Road, 138
Brown's Inlet, 63
Brown's Mountains, 22, 25
Brown's Tract, 20, 22, 23, 24, 25, 39, 61, 67, 73
Buck Hill, 97
Buck Pond, 126, 142
Buffalo, 13, 143
Bull Rock, 139
Bull Run Road, 138
Bullhead Pond, 89, 137
Bullpout Pond, 137
Bum Pond, 33, 136, 137, 148
Bump Road, 138
Burnt Hill, 97
Buttocks Hill, 139

Calamity Pond, 31, 73, 75, 89
Canistaguaha (see Half Moon), 103
Cascade Mountain, 95
Castor, 53
Castorland, 18, 29, 53, 54, 109

Catskills, 16, 110
Champlain Valley, 111
Charlotte County, 31
Charlottesboro, 55, 58
Chateaugay, 49
Chazy, 29, 71
Chevrolet Road, 138
Chicago, 41, 70, 103
Chi-Gon-Der-O-Ga (see Ticonderoga), 40, 101
Chub River, 68, 69, 73, 74
Cicero, 143
Clarksboro, 145
Clear Pond, 124, 127, 128, 148
Cliff Mountain, 95
Clinton County, Iowa, 27
Clinton County, New York, 29, 31, 59, 97, 111, 135, 137, 138
Cobble Hill, 48
Cockold Town, 139
Coffee Pond, 148
Coffins Mills, 145
Cold River, 85
Coney Island, 29, 110
Conifer, 145
Connecticut, 69
Connestigune (see Niskayuna), 103
Copper Kill Pond, 91, 111
Corbeau Creek, 109
Corduroy Road, 137
Corinth, 143
Cork, 144
Corlear Bay, 18
Corlear Mountains, 18, 20, 25
Couchsachraga Peak, 96
Couchsachrage, The Antient, 18, 20, 21, 25, 26, 37, 42, 50, 55, 109
Cranberry Lake, 32
Cranberry Pond, 126
Cream of the Valley Road, 33, 138
Crobar Road, 138
Crusher Road, 138
Crystal Brook, 89
Cumberland Head, 55

Dakota, 100, 122
Dandy Road, 138
Dannemora, 25, 60, 111
Dark and Bloody Ground, The, 20, 22, 26

Day Care Mountain, 136
Deer Pond, 126
DeGrasse, 108
DePeyster, 108
Deserted Village, The, 74
Devil's Den Road, 138
Devil's Oven, 148
Devil's Pulpit, 33, 82, 83, 148
Devil's Wash Dish, 142, 148
Dial Mountain, 95, 97
Diana, 32, 109, 143
Dibble Hollow, 97
Dippkill Pond, 91, 111
Dippikill Mountain, 111
Dismal Swamp, 20
Dismal Wilderness, The, 20, 26
Dix Mountain, 95
Doctor Hill, 97
Doctors Lake, 144
Dollar Road, 138
Donnelly Brook, 91
Drunkard Creek, 33
Dry Lake, 136, 137
Duane, 30
Dunk Pond, 148
Dutch West Indies, The, 15, 62

E'Town (see Elizabethtown), 54
Eagle Eyrie, 145
East Dix, 95
Easy Street, 27, 84
Economy, 63
Eddy Mountain, 97
Elbow Pond, 89
Elizabethtown, 30, 54, 55, 58, 64, 65, 67, 97
Empire State, The, 14
Enterprise, 63
Essex, 31, 44, 48, 54, 60, 64, 73, 80, 104, 113, 135, 136, 137, 143, 148
Esther Mountain, 95, 96
Eureka, 135
Ezraville, 49

Fairy Ladder Falls, 148
Fawn Ridge, 145
First Lake, 114
Follensby Pond, 88
Fort Apache, 29
Fort Schuyler, 63, 68, 131

4-H Road, 138
Francis Hill, 97
Franklin County, 31, 49, 59, 90, 101, 131, 135, 136
French Hill, 110, 145
French Pond, 91
French Road, 110
French Settlement Road, 109
Frenchmans Creek, 91
Frenchs Brook, 91
French's Hollow, 110
Frenchs Vly, 91
Frenchtown, 110, 138
Frenette Mountain, 109
Frog Hollow, 114
Frugality, 63
Fulton Chain, The, 20, 31, 37, 38, 39, 40, 61, 63, 67, 114, 115, 116
Fulton County, 59, 135, 136

Gabriels, 83
Galilee, 32, 64
Galway, 144
Giant Mountain, 95, 97
Gizzle Ocean Mountain, 97, 126, 136, 148
Glenburnie, 113
Glendale, 145
Glens Falls, 13
Golden Pond, 142
Golly Road, 138
Gothic Mountain, 95, 97
Gougeville, 64, 81
Gougeville Spring Road, 137
Gouverneur, 30
Granville, 135
Grass Pond, 89, 126
Grassy Pond, 143
Gray Peak, 95
Great Tract No. 1 (to 6), 50, 51, 53
Great Tract No. 5, 53, 68
Grizzle Ocean Pond, 27, 33, 137, 148
Grog Harbor, 33, 148
Guay Creek, 109

Hague, 31, 60, 144
Half Moon, 29, 103, 110
Hamilton County, 59, 91, 105. 113, 135, 136

Harison, 49
Harrietstown, 66
Hatirondacks (see Adirondacks), 24
Hays Brook, 88
Haystack Mountain, 95
Hazard Road, 137, 138
Helldiver Pond, 136, 137
Hell's Kitchen Road, 137
Herefordshire, 148
Herkimer County, 136, 137, 138
Hills of Hebron, 148
Hodenosauneega (see People of the Long House), 16, 20, 25
Hogansburg, 30
Homer, 143
Honey Pond, 148
Hooper Dooper Road, 138
Hot Water Pond, 33, 89, 137, 148
Hough Peak, 95
Hudson River, 24, 56, 92, 93
Hudson Valley, 18, 29, 54, 55, 110
Huletts Station, 145
Humbug Brook, 136, 137

Ilion, 32, 143
Illinois, 141, 142
Indian Brook, 90
Indian Creek, 90
Indian Falls, 90
Indian Lake, 90
Indian Mountain, 90
Indian Pass, 74, 90
Indian Point, 90, 103, 139
Indian River, 90
Indian Rock, 103
Indian Trail, 103
Industry, 63
Irish Brook, 91
Irish Settlement Road, 138
Irishtown, 99, 144, 145
Iroquois Peak, 90, 96, 100
Iroquoisia, 16, 19, 20, 25
Ithaca, 143

Jamesboro, 55, 58
Jefferson County, 59, 135
Jenny Lake, 89
Jericho, 32, 64
Jerusalem, 32
Jerusalem Road, 64

Jimmy Creek, 88
Joe Indian Outlet, 90
Joe Indian Pond, 90
Joe Pond, 142
Johns Brook, 88
Jordan River, 64
Jug Mountain, 97, 148
Jug Pond, 148

Kansas Road, 138
Kattskill Bay, 111
Kayaderosseras, 103, 104
Kays Hill, 97
Keene Valley, 47, 85
Keeseville, 30, 109, 110, 143
Kennedy, 31
Kentucky, 20
Kickerville, 64, 81
Kiln Brook, 112
Kitty Cobble, 97
Kiwassa, 28, 102
Klondike Brook, 31, 148
Knappville, 145
Knowersville, 27, 33
Kokomo Corners, 135
Konoshion, 16, 20, 25
Kushaqua, 102

La Duke Road, 110
La Flesh Road, 110
La Rock, 91
La Rue Road, 110
Labrador, 15
Lac du Sacrement (see Lake George),
    42, 73, 93, 108
Lac du Skaroon (see Schroon Lake),
    108
Lake Algonquin, 90
Lake Bonaparte, 109
Lake Champlain, 13, 16, 18, 25, 29,
    31, 39, 40, 41, 55, 56, 57, 60, 71, 72,
    73, 74, 93, 104, 105, 107, 108, 131,
    142, 144
Lake Chartreuse, 109
Lake Erie, 103
Lake Flower, 31, 59, 65, 94
Lake George, 29, 31, 39, 42, 55, 56, 72,
    73, 83, 89, 93, 108, 113, 131, 142
Lake Lila, 30, 89
Lake Ontario, 13

Lake Placid Village, 14, 32, 47, 61, 67,
    68, 69, 70, 73, 113, 146, 147
Lake Serenity, 141
Lake Tear-of-the-Clouds, 148
Lamora Mountain, 109
Laphams Mills, 144
Larry Ryan Mountain, 97
Lawrence Brook, 88
Lawyer Mountain, 136
Le Bridge Road, 110
Le Goys Brook, 109
Le Roux Road, 99
LeRayville, 30
Lesperance Mountain, 109
Lewis County, 89, 135, 137
Lily Pad Pond, 126, 132
Lily Pond, 32
Lisbon, 144
Little Chicago, 68, 70
Loch Bonnie, 29, 99, 113, 148
Loch Mueller, 113
Loch Muller, 113
Lock Miller Road, 113
Lonesome Pond, 33
Long Island, 29, 49
Long Lake, 32, 64, 124, 130
Long Pond, 124, 130
Long Sue, 97
Look, 148
Loon Lake, 89
Lost Mountain, 97
Lost Nation Road, 64
Lost Pond, 124, 129, 148
Louisville, 108
Lower Wolf Jaw Mountain, 95
Lydia Pond, 89
Lyon Mountain, 25

Macomb Mountains, The, 20, 25
Madrid, 60, 64, 144
Maidenhead, 139
Malone, 49, 50, 53, 64, 144
Man Cow Rock, 139
Manhattan, 53, 103
Manlius, 143
Massachusetts, 60
Massena, 143
Massena Springs, 105
McBride Pond, 88
McComb Mountain, 95

Meacham Lake, 30
Mexico, 31, 60
Milton, 60
Minerva, 32, 143, 144
Mirror Lake, 32
Mississippi River, 103, 144
Moffitsville, 144
Mohawk Ridge, 90
Mohawk River, 13, 24, 61, 68, 131
Mohawk Valley, 18, 131
Monongahela, 143
Montauk, 100
Montauk Point, 100
Montreal, 13, 18, 71, 72, 76
Moody's (see The Pines), 66
Moonshine Pond, 33
Moose River, 38
Moriah, 64
Moses Kill, 91, 111
Moshier Falls, 145
Mossy, 148
Mount Clinton, 95
Mount Colden, 95
Mount Colvin, 95
Mount Donaldson, 95, 97
Mount Electra, 32
Mount Emmons, 95
Mount Etna, 32
Mount Marcy, 22, 31, 58, 59, 64, 95, 97, 100, 104
Mount Overrocker, 136
Mount Pisgah, 32, 47, 48, 49, 50, 53, 63, 64, 142, 148, 149
Mount Redfield, 95
Mount St. Louis, 116
Mount Skylight, 95
Mount Tom, 97
Mount Van Hoevenberg, 113
Mountains of St. Marthe, 18, 20, 25
Mountainview, 32
Muck Road, 137
Mud Pond, 32, 121, 124, 128, 131, 143, 148

Nancy Ryan Mountain, 97
Napoleon's Cap, 148
Nehasane, 106, 115
New England, 15, 56, 60, 69, 122
New France (see Avacal), 15, 16, 53, 108

New Netherlands (see Novi Belgii), 16
New Russia, 31, 60
New Spain, 15
New Street, 33
New Sweden, 60, 110, 111, 112
New York City, 13, 16, 29, 38, 52, 53, 54, 55, 58, 62, 68, 77, 103, 110
New York State, 15, 16, 27, 52, 53, 58, 61, 69, 104, 120, 122, 123, 124, 143
New York Wilderness, The, 22, 25
Newton Falls, 145
Niagara Falls, 93, 148, 149
Nick Mountain, 97
Niggerhead Mountain, 139
Nihanawate, 106
Nippletop Mountain, 95, 97, 139, 143
Niskayuna, 103
North Branch, 32
North Country, The, 20, 22, 25, 125
North Elba Township, 14, 20, 61, 69
North Granville Truthville, 135
North Pole, 148
North Woods, The, 20, 25
Northampton, 144
Northern Wilderness, The, 22, 25
Norway, 31, 60, 144
Novi Belgii, 16, 20, 25
Nye Mountain, 95

O K Slip Brook, 136, 137
O K Slip Falls, 148
Ohio, 143
Old Forge, 39, 67
Old Street, 33
Olmstedville, 144
Onchiota, 28, 90, 102, 144
Oneida County, 135, 137
Onoville, 27
Oseetah, 102
Oswegatchie, 28, 85, 105
Ouleout Creek, 91
Overshot Pond, 137
Owl Kill, 91

Pack Horse Mountain, 148
Panther Peak, 95

Paradox Lake, 133
Parts, 135
Paul Smiths, 30, 83
Peach Blow Hill, 97
Pepper Hollow, 148
Perseverance, 63
Peru, 16, 40, 144
Peru Mountains (see Peruvian
    Mountains), 16
Peruvian Mountains, 16, 20, 25
Peters Corners, 145
Peters Pond, 88
Pharaoh Mountain, 32, 148
Phelix Road, 110, 112
Phelps Mountain, 95
Phoebe Mountain, 97
Pierrepont, 108
Pine Pond, 126
Plains of Abraham, 69
Plank Bridge Hill, 97
Plank Road, 137
Plattsburgh, 25, 29, 30, 44, 55, 71, 72,
    83, 90, 105, 110, 113, 142
Pleasant Valley, 48
Podunk Brook, 106, 136
Podunk Road, 107
Poke-O-Moonshine Mountain, 104,
    148
Poker Pond, 33
Poland, 144
Polack Pond, 139
Polliwog Pond, 89
Poor Road, 138
Pork Barrel Pond, 136, 137
Port Kent, 144
Porter Mountain, 95
Potsdam, 105, 107
Pottersville, 145
Prima Vista, 15, 16, 20, 25
Pru (see Peru), 40
Pudding Hollow, 148
Pulpit Rock, 148
Pyramid Lakes, 148

Quaker Mountain, 148
Quebec, 13, 75, 92, 112
Quicksand Outlet, 141

Radar Road, 138
Rainbow Bower, 149

Rainbow Lake, 102
Raquette Lake, 41, 43, 67, 100, 106
Raquette River, 29, 41, 43, 88, 106,
    107, 142
Ratinonsionni (see Adirondacks), 24
Ratirontaks (see Adirondacks), 24
Rattlesnake Knob, 145
Regularity, 63
Rensselaerswick, 16
Riverview, 32
Riverview Heights, 145
Roaring Brook, 32
Rock Lake, 89
Rock Pond, 126
Rock Road, 137
Rocky Peak Ridge, 95
Rodunk Brook, 136, 137
Rogers' Rock, 83
Rome, 148
Rondaxe, 24
Rondaxe Mountain, 114, 116
Rooseveltown, 31
Round Pond, 124
Russia, 144
Russian Lake, 91

S'nhalo'nek (see Saranac River), 66,
    105
Sabattis, 42, 100
Sabbath Day Point, 31, 64, 89
Saddleback Mountain, 95
St. Aranack (see Saranac), 66
St. Armand (see Saranac), 66
St. Lawrence County, 20, 31, 82, 105,
    113, 131, 135, 137, 138
St. Lawrence River, 13, 15, 40, 42, 56,
    85, 92, 93, 101, 107, 131
St. Lawrence Valley, 20, 50
St. Louis, Missouri, 114, 115, 116
St. Margaret Mountains, 18, 20, 25
St. Martin (see Saranac), 66
St. Regis Falls, 77
Saints Rest, 148
Salasanac (see Saranac River), 66
Sally's Rock, 81, 82
Salmon River, 32, 55, 88
Salonak (see Saranac River), 66
Santa Clara, 31, 60, 75, 76, 77, 144
Santanoni Peak, 96
Saranac River, 44, 73, 88, 94, 101, 102,

105, 110, 111, 132, 144
Saranac Lake Village, 14, 36, 47, 59, 65, 66, 67, 90, 93, 94, 102, 136
Saratoga, 28, 41, 60, 90, 104, 111, 135, 136, 138, 144
Savaniac (see Saranac River), 66
Schenectady, 28
Sawteeth Mountain, 95, 96
Schroon Lake, 29, 93, 104, 107, 108, 113, 114
Schroon River, 142
Schuyler Falls, 29
Scotch Bonnet, 29, 113
Scotch Lake, 91, 113
Scotch Settlement Road, 113
Scuttle Hole Creek, 33
Second Lake, 115
Seneca, 143
Serindac (see Saranac River), 66
Seward Mountain, 95
Seymour Mountain, 95
Shanty Bottom Brook, 148
Shenandoah, 144
Short Road, 138
Siberia of North America, The, 26
Sink Hole, 27, 83
Sitting Bull Road, 138
Skanetaghrowahna (see Schroon Lake), 104
Sknoonapus (see Schroon Lake), 104
Skunk Hollow, 141
Slab City, 32, 135
Slang Pond, 137
Sly Pond, 136, 137
Smith Kill Brook, 111
Snook Kill, 91
Sober Kiln, 33, 148
Sobriety, 27, 63
Sodom, 32, 64
South Dix, 95
South Granville, 135
South Meadow, 32
South Woods, The, 20, 25
Sporting Hill, 136
Squaw Brook, 90
Squaw Creek, 90
Squaw Lake, 90
Stammer Road, 137
Starbuckville, 145

Staten Island, 139
Stella Mountain, 97
Stink Hole, 44, 46, 101
Stockholm, 144
Stone Road, 137
Street Mountain, 95
Sugarbush, 143
Sunday Creek, 31
Sunday Swamp, 89
Susquehanna, 143
Syracuse, 13, 44, 101, 105, 143

Tabletop Mountain, 95, 96
Tahawus (see Mount Marcy), 28, 58, 95, 104, 144
Tanawadeh (see Raquette), 106
Tatirontaks (see Adirondacks), 24
Tea Cup Road, 138
Tewatenetarenies (see Potsdam), 105
Texas Ridge, 148
The Pines, 66
The River (see Saranac Village), 66
Thendara, 38
Thomas Hill, 97
Thurman, 145
Ti (see Ticonderoga), 40, 41, 101
Ticonderoga, 28, 39, 41, 90, 92, 114, 143, 144
Tight Nipping, 33, 126, 148
Timbuktu, 61, 68, 70, 73, 145, 148
Tonawanda, 144
Toothaker Road, 137
Toowarloondah (see Blue Mountain Lake), 144
Top Notch Road, 137
Totten and Crossfield Purchase, 23
Trout Brook, 89
Troy, 122, 143
Trudeau (see Saranac Lake Village), 66
Tupper Lake, 30, 33, 61, 64, 75, 76, 81, 82, 88
Turtle Pond, 36, 37, 44

Unanimity, 63
Unknown Pond, 136, 137
Up The River (see Saranac Lake Village), 27, 66
Upper Duck Hole, 89
Upper Wolf Jaw Mountain, 95

Utica, 13, 37, 39, 63, 76, 77, 105, 131

Valcour Island, 56
Valley of the Ausable, The, 69
Van Derwacker Pond, 91
Vermontville, 31, 60, 83, 110
Vice Road, 138
Vly Creek, 112

Warm Pond, 148
Warren County, 31, 111, 135, 136, 138
Washington County, 31, 59, 64, 106, 111, 135, 136, 138
Watertown, 109

Watervliet, 29, 110
Wawbeek, 144
Wells, 145
West Granville Corners, 135
Westport, 55
Whippleville, 144
Whiteface Mountain, 32, 95, 96, 97
Willsboro, 30, 54, 55, 58, 97
Wolf Creek, 89
Wolf Pond, 32
Wright Peak, 95
Why Pond, 136, 137

Yonkers, 110

Zurich, 144

Index of Maps and Schematics

Adirondacks, The, 123
Avacal (*Theatrum Orbis Terrarum of 1575*), 17

Blue Line, The, 125
British Colonial American Map of 1755, 21
Brown's Tract, 23

Clear Ponds, 127, 128

Gilliland Estates, 57

Long Lakes, 130
Long Ponds, 130
Lost Ponds, 129

Macomb Purchase, 23, 51
Mud Ponds, 121, 128

New Netherlands Map of 1616, 19
New York State, 123

Totten and Crossfield Purchase, 23

Selected Reading

This list represents those books which proved of particular interest and value to me for the writing of *Call Me Adirondack*. There are a great many other valuable and pleasurable books about the Adirondacks, and I recommend a quiet browse through Dorothy Plum's *Adirondack Bibliography*. I have indicated the publisher and date of publication only when the book is not available in a current printing.

Regional and County Histories

A History of the Adirondacks, Alfred L. Donaldson.
Adirondack Country, William C. White.
The History of Lake Champlain, Peter S. Palmer.
The North Country, A History, Harry F. Landon (Historical Printing Co, 1932).
The Adirondacks, Fulton Chain, Joseph F. Grady (Journal and Courier Co., 1933).
History of St. Lawrence and Franklin Counties, Franklin B. Hough.
Military and Civil History of the County of Essex, Winslow C. Watson (J. Munsell, 1869).
Township 34, Harold Hochschild.

Folklore and Names

Aboriginal Place Names of New York, William M. Beauchamp (New York State Museum Bulletin, 1907).
Body, Boots and Britches, Harold W. Thompson.
Names On The Land, George R. Stewart.